C000279627

Promoting Individual and Organisational Learning in Social Work

Promoting Individual and Organisational Learning in Social Work

SARAH WILLIAMS
LYNNE RUTTER
IVAN GRAY

Series Editor: Keith Brown

Learning Matters
An imprint of SAGE Publications Ltd
1 Oliver's Yard
55 City Road
London EC1Y 1SP

SAGE Publications Inc.
2455 Teller Road
Thousand Oaks, California 91320

SAGE Publications India Pvt Ltd
B 1/I 1 Mohan Cooperative Industrial Area
Mathura Road
New Delhi 110 044

SAGE Publications Asia-Pacific Pte Ltd
3 Church Street
#10-04 Samsung Hub
Singapore 049483

Editor: Luke Block
Development editor: Lauren Simpson
Production controller: Chris Marke
Project management: Swales & Willis Ltd, Exeter, Devon
Marketing manager: Tamara Navaratnam
Cover design: Wendy Scott
Typeset by: Swales & Willis Ltd, Exeter, Devon
Printed by: MPG Books Group, Bodmin, Cornwall

© 2012 Sarah Williams, Lynne Rutter, Ivan Gray

First published 2012

Apart from any fair dealing for the purposes of research or private study, or criticism or review, as permitted under the Copyright, Design and Patents Act, 1988, this publication may be reproduced, stored or transmitted in any form, or by any means, only with the prior permission in writing of the publishers, or in the case of reprographic reproduction, in accordance with the terms of licences issued by the Copyright Licensing Agency. Enquiries concerning reproduction outside these terms should be sent to the publishers.

Library of Congress Control Number: 2012945180

British Library Cataloguing in Publication Data

A catalogue record for this book is available from the British Library

ISBN 9781446266908
ISBN 9781446266915 (pbk)

MIX
Paper from
responsible sources
FSC
www.fsc.org   FSC® C018575

Contents

List of illustrations and activities

Figures

Tables

Activities

About the authors

Sarah Williams has been employed in senior and middle management positions in a range of statutory, voluntary and independent sector organisations. She has a particular interest in the development of professional capability through work-based learning and has 18 years' experience as a practice educator and 12 years' experience as a senior lecturer. Sarah currently works at Bournemouth University, where she is the co-ordinator of the Practice Educator Programme and also a contributor to leadership and management education. She is co-author of the Learning Matters text *The Practice Educator's Handbook*.

Lynne Rutter holds academic and professional qualifications in education and has several years' experience of developing and delivering Bournemouth University programmes. Her doctorate research focused on the development of professional knowledge and she is a co-author of the Learning Matters texts *Critical Thinking and Professional Judgement for Social Work* and *The Practice Educator's Handbook*. Currently she is developing continuing professional development units for post-qualifying social work.

Ivan Gray holds academic and professional qualifications in social work and management and specialises in management development. Before his retirement in 2012 he was programme leader for the BA in Health and Social Care Management and MA in Leading and Developing Services at Bournemouth University.

Foreword

In today's performance driven and managerialist environment, maintaining service quality in social work is more important than ever. This book is intended to help managers and social workers understand the fundamental role that professional and organisational learning plays in the provision of services that are effective and responsive to the needs of service users, carers and the communities in which they live. Recent national policy drivers such as the Munro report (2011) and the recommendations of the Social Work Reform Board (2010) strengthen the importance of embedding and enabling learning within the workplace and, although professional learning is the responsibility of all employees, managers have a special role to play.

This book will help managers to explore how they can fulfil this role at both a strategic and operational level. In response to the Munro report (2011), the government has called for a change in the way that social services are delivered. At the heart of these changes is an understanding that risk cannot be eliminated and an expectation that front-line practitioners will be given more freedom to exercise their professional judgement. If such changes are to be made, managers will need to have the skills and confidence to create a climate in which critical reflection on practice is encouraged and supported, and where a commitment to continuous learning and improvement is the norm. This text provides opportunities for managers to consider ways in which they can foster and develop learning at an individual, group and organisational level, allowing practitioners to commit to maximise the effectiveness of their practice which, in turn, enhances the quality of the service.

The primary aims of this book are to:

- help managers to respond to the key recommendations of the Social Work Reform Board (2010) and the Munro report (2011) with regard to learning and development;

- focus on the essential need for leading and enabling continued learning and professional development for maintaining/improving service quality;

- identify and explore the use of learning cultures and partnership approaches for leading and enabling such learning.

As with all the post-qualifying social work texts, this book is written and designed to ensure that the very best social work practice is delivered within our society and, with this aim in mind, I highly commend this text to you.

Professor Keith Brown
Series Editor
Director of the Centre for Post Qualifying Social Work,
Bournemouth University

Introduction

As we are writing this book the social work profession is facing one of the most significant shake-ups in its history. Following a decline in public and government confidence, the Social Work Reform Board (SWRB) was established in 2010 to look at how social workers and the agencies that employed them could respond to the recommendations of the Social Work Task Force (SWTF, 2009) and make their services fit for purpose in the twenty-first century. Work is now in progress to turn the recommendations into practical solutions that will enable social workers to deliver cost-effective and responsive services that safeguard and support the most vulnerable members of our society.

In essence, the SWRB has developed recommendations to establish a Professional Capabilities Framework (PCF), employer standards and a framework for continuing professional development. A new College of Social Work is now fully responsible for the PCF, introduced in 2012 as the single way in which social workers should think about and plan their careers and professional development. The College says the PCF is a 'living' document, in that it is likely to develop as the profession develops, serving as a backdrop to both initial social work education (an assessed and supported year in employment or ASYE), and continuing professional development after qualification.

At the heart of the reform agenda is the recognition that social workers practise in uncertain and complex situations in which risk can never be completely eliminated. Both the SWRB and the more recently published Munro report (2011) stress the importance of moving away from top-down, target-driven management towards a more creative and flexible approach to service provision that enables social workers to learn from their experiences and have more freedom to exercise their professional judgement.

In this book we aim to show that improvements to individual and organisational learning set against a backdrop of improved cultures for learning are not just a desirable part of the reform of social work but an essential foundation on which to build the recommended changes. If social workers are to be given more freedom to exercise professional judgement they must be encouraged and supported to think for themselves and make situation-responsive, evidence-informed judgements. Learning is therefore not just something that happens at the beginning of a career or in an occasional training course, which quickly becomes a low priority or even stops. Learning should be something that happens every time a social worker speaks to a service user, works alongside another professional, engages in supervision or encounters any new situation. Social workers' knowledge and skills must evolve over time to ensure that they keep pace with new developments and are flexible enough to respond to unexpected and complex situations. It follows that if real change is to happen within the profession, all social workers must be encouraged to take personal responsibility for keeping up to date and for critically reflecting on their experiences to gain a deeper understanding of how they can provide a more effective service.

However, improving the way that individual social workers learn is only half the story because services are provided within an organisational context. Individual learning must therefore be shared and developed in order to inform the knowledge and skill base of organisations as a whole. Taking an organisational approach to learning places service users' and carers' needs at the centre of reform because it ensures that the people at the front line with direct experience of providing services are able to learn from each other and provide managers and policy makers with valuable insights into what works and doesn't work in practice. Improving the way that organisations learn will, in many cases, require major shifts in attitude and approach from people working at all levels, but most particularly from those with leadership and management responsibilities who are in a position to drive forward the necessary changes and create a culture in which all forms of learning can thrive.

This book has been designed to help leaders and managers of people delivering social care to evaluate realistically the culture for learning that currently exists within their organisations and to begin to explore ideas and formulate plans that will bring about concrete and achievable improvements.

How to use this book

This book is intended to introduce you to some key ideas to support you in your leading or enabling role. It is not a textbook in the sense that it will refer to the complete range of theory or research on a topic, nor will it tell you what to do. As mentioned in the introduction, we are dealing with complex and uncertain issues that do not have simple solutions, and any options need to be considered in relation to your own organisation and professional context. Although this book has been written by three authors, a consistent approach has been taken to direct and stimulate your thinking around a selection of relevant (but not exhaustive) issues.

The experience of facilitating learning in practice, the critical evaluation of this practice together with any structured learning can help you to develop your wider professional capabilities as a designated leader or manager. The particular approaches or styles of leadership that are likely to be most effective for learning and development situations need to be considered throughout this textbook. Think about what your preferred leadership style is and whether you need to adapt this for the particular contexts and needs we discuss.

We provide activities that prompt you to consider the ways in which you can lead, foster and develop learning at an individual, group and organisational level. You can explore each topic in greater depth by following recommendations for further reading that have been included at the end of each chapter. You could also access specific training to help you to develop relevant skills further.

Section One concentrates on understanding more about the particular type of learning and development taking place in a workplace environment, plus how and why organisations and people learn. It can help you to become a more critically reflective leader/enabler of learning through gaining a greater insight into your own and the learning and development of others.

In Section Two we help you to explore how you can fulfil an enabling role at both strategic and operational levels in a number of different situations – e.g. induction, supervision, meetings, case reviews.

Section 1

Chapter 1
Learning organisations

We live in a world in which complexity and rapid change are the norm and in which new technologies have revolutionised the way we communicate, gain knowledge and live our everyday lives. Social, cultural, demographic and economic changes have resulted in many of us living in diverse and rapidly evolving communities which have complex expectations and needs (Cherry, 2005). This poses significant challenges to health and social care organisations that are tasked with providing responsive services in a climate in which there are increasing pressures on resources and where there is an expectation that patients, service users and carers will play a greater role in the design and evaluation of the services that they receive.

A culture of learning

People at all levels in service-providing organisations need to be able to keep pace with change, have confidence in dealing with uncertainty and the mechanisms in place to ensure that there is a good understanding of the needs of the community (Nixon and Murr, 2006). This means that knowledge and understanding become key components for effective practice and as a result learning should be inherent and continuous. In its final report the Social Work Reform Board (SWRB, 2010) acknowledges the responsibility the organisation has here for developing and actively supporting a strong learning culture.

The Munro report (Munro, 2011) goes further by understanding that the more usual and dominant culture of compliance in such organisations needs to be dealt with first. It recommends a:

> radical reduction in the amount of central prescription to help professionals move from a compliance culture to a learning culture, where they have more freedom to use their expertise in assessing need and providing the right help.

> (Munro, 2011: 6–7)

In effect, the key idea here is that managing the uncertain world of practice is best undertaken within a culture of professional learning and development because a culture of control and compliance is likely to hinder that learning. An organisation which sees the need to find ways to control people so that they do not make mistakes puts huge psychological pressure on people. This style of management reduces the scope for individual judgement by adding procedures and rules, and increases monitoring to ensure compliance with these rules. In the end it produces a heavily bureaucratised and ineffective system, which creates obstacles to good practice and prioritises the demands of performance management over service users' needs (Munro, 2011). As Munro explains further, any perceived defence and security of 'following correct procedures' is actually false, as it *creates a feedback loop that reinforces the defensive routine based on a procedural perspective* which *hampers professional learning* and stifles the development of expertise (Munro, 2011: 20). Munro recognises that a better understanding of the nature of health and social care practice is required which acknowledges the emotional dimensions and intellectual nuances of professional reasoning. These, in turn, need to be valued, shared and developed within and across organisations to enable high-quality services. Allowing professionals greater opportunity for responsible innovation and space for professional judgement therefore seems a fundamental tenet for any learning organisation.

Of course, procedures can also be the product of a learning organisation, i.e. as a pre-determined plan of action that limits professional discretion and choices on the basis of previous organisational experiences. Crucially, however, this also means that the development and application of procedures by a learning organisation (as distinct from a bureaucracy) would display a number of features.

- In a learning organisation procedures are used sparingly and to target activities that need to be controlled to eliminate risk for professionals and people who use services, or ensure fairness and good governance.

- There is an awareness of the potential negative impact of procedures on organisational learning and practice.

- The reasons for introducing a procedure, i.e. the objectives of the procedure, are clear.

- There is an awareness that procedures have their limitations and that situations can sometimes arise when they should not be followed.

- The need to preserve professional discretion is accepted as a principle so that procedures are introduced with reluctance following consultation and ensuring professional ownership.

- Procedures are regularly reviewed and improved or, if possible, dropped.

How can organisations learn?

In effect, a culture of learning at both an organisational and an individual level is of vital importance if the organisation as a whole is to respond to change and provide high-quality services. But how does an organisation learn and what is the role of the leader here? Essentially, there needs to be a fundamental capacity for 'bottom-up', 'across' and 'top-down' learning via a flow of information and ideas. On a day-to-day basis the workings of complex practices and multi-agency services require monitoring. Service user and staff experiences need to feed into a wider knowledge base; staff need to share information, learn together and develop a shared understanding; and there needs to be a good flow of information about key decisions. Developing and enabling such networks or pathways, therefore, becomes a critical role for leaders and managers. In addition, new processes and innovations can have unexpected consequences as they are put into operation and interact with other parts of the system, so good feedback structures at all levels are needed to notice any emerging problems and quickly address them.

Munro (2011) also recommends adopting a recent healthcare emphasis on understanding human error rather than seeking to eradicate it. After consulting with a number of local authorities which sought to increase the knowledge and skills of their workforce and to create less prescriptive working environments, she found they were creating learning cultures where change was expected as a consequence of that learning. Their receptiveness to regular feedback from the front line helped to create an adaptive environment with greater opportunity to exercise appropriate professional judgement (Munro, 2011: 133).

Learning organisations can, therefore, provide structures and cultures that foster useful and effective learning pathways, for example by:

- enhancing employee, patient, service user and care involvement in planning and evaluating services;

- supporting team work and networking (within and outside organisational boundaries);

- promoting openness, creativity, experimentation;

- encouraging members to acquire, process and share information;

- providing freedom to try new things, make mistakes and learn from experience.

Peter Senge's model

The business world has long recognised that in situations of rapid change the organisations that are most likely to thrive are those that are flexible and adaptive. Peter Senge (1990) argued that a fundamental requirement for this was that people at all levels within an organisation were both enthusiastic about learning and enabled to learn effectively. Furthermore, he proposed that the most successful organisations will not only adapt their behaviour to cope with changes that have already happened but will be creative and forward-looking to ensure that they can continue to be responsive and meet the challenges of the future. It was Senge who described organisations capable of both adapting to change and being creative as *learning organisations*.

Senge (1990) identified five basic *disciplines* that needed to be mastered if an organisation was going to become a learning organisation:

1. systems thinking;

2. personal mastery;

3. mental models;

4. building shared vision;

5. team thinking.

We can explore these elements further to help understand and adapt key principles to work towards.

Systems thinking

Systems thinking is at the heart of all effective learning organisations. Senge (1990) believed that many organisations are too simplistic in the way they approach management, seeking the most obvious short-term solutions and failing to recognise the complex relationships between different aspects of an organisation's functioning. For example, cutting back on training budgets can lead to immediate cost savings when resources are limited but will almost inevitably be very costly in the longer term as the skills base of the staff drops and employees feel devalued. A grasp of systems theory and an ability to picture the systems that make up an organisation together with an ability to view the impact of actions over a longer timescale are seen as crucial to the development and maintenance of a learning organisation. Although senior and strategic managers have a central role in ensuring that systems thinking is used as a basis for planning, Senge believed that it is important that people at all levels within an organisation are supported to develop 'systems thinking' to ensure that this way of working permeates all areas of the organisation's work.

Personal mastery

Personal mastery is a term coined by Senge (1990) to describe a state of being in which individuals are most effective as learners. It is important in the development of a learning organisation because organisations can only learn if the individuals who make up the organisation are able to learn effectively. People with high levels of personal mastery have all of the attributes and skills necessary to make them highly effective learners. They are open to learning and are aware of their own learning needs. They recognise the need for lifelong learning and are humble but self-confident as learners. According to Senge, learning organisations need to support individuals to develop their personal mastery and grow as learners.

Mental models

Mental models are the ways that we make sense of the world around us, the set of assumptions that we have learnt to make to help us deal with the information overload that the world presents. They are helpful as a way of coping with life but can close our minds to alternative viewpoints and thwart personal growth and development. We are not often consciously aware of the assumptions that we make or of their impact on our behaviour. However, for individuals to learn from their experiences they need to be able to uncover these assumptions and hold them up to scrutiny, allowing their thinking to be influenced by others and opening their minds to new ideas. Entrenched mental models (i.e. always doing something the same way because it is the way that it has always been done) can be a significant block to effective action that has been identified through systems thinking, and so bringing about changes to the way that individuals within organisations think is an essential element of the development of an effective learning organisation. These ideas are closely allied to the concept of reflective practice, which also stresses the importance of self-awareness and uncovering assumptions (Schön, 1992; Moon, 1999; Gould and Baldwin, 2004; Thompson, 2006).

Building shared vision

Building shared vision with all members of an organisation helps to ensure that people learn, develop and create not because they are told to but because they want to. Learning organisations need to work towards a situation where there is a clear and shared vision of what the organisation is trying to achieve to which individuals can contribute and reinforce.

Team thinking

Team thinking is the last of the disciplines described by Senge (1990) and describes the ability of individuals genuinely to work and think together to enable them to gain insights that would not be possible for them thinking alone. An important part of the success of team thinking is being able to recognise the blocks to effective team thinking and put in place strategies which support effective team working.

In effect, learning organisations need new types of leaders who can take responsibility for creating and building a shared vision, for putting in place strategies for supporting and enabling individual and team growth, encouraging individuals to become involved in decision making and to take leadership responsibilities in their areas of strength or expertise (Hafford-Letchfield *et al.*, 2008).

ACTIVITY **1.1**

Your organisation

How well do these disciplines fit into a hierarchical, outcomes-driven organisation like a health authority or a social services department?

To what extent do you honestly believe that you and the team in which you work have mastered the above disciplines?

Can you think of one simple thing that you could do to help you or your team develop in each of the above areas?

A major criticism of Senge's work is that, although theoretically the benefits of working in this way are clear, very few organisations come even close to meeting all of the criteria. So why do organisations struggle to achieve this ideal? There are clearly some significant tensions between the ways of working that would need to be in place to support the development of Senge's vision of a learning organisation and more traditional approaches to management and leadership. Also, the concept of the learning organisation can be seen as an oversimplification which fails to take into account the complex nature of the relationships between individuals that exist within organisations, or indeed the external pressures such as government targets and initiatives that are imposed on organisations from outside. Nyhan *et al.* (2003, cited by Gould and Baldwin, 2004) point out that if an organisation is to be able to respond to change it must evolve and constantly reinvent itself, and this does not fit well with a formulaic notion of a learning organisation. They propose that, instead of attempting to apply the same learning organisation formula, each organisation needs to find its own unique response. Therefore, although Senge's ideas have been highly influential, it is debatable that his vision of a learning organisation is achievable in a large and complex organisation such as a local authority (Thompson, 2006).

Nevertheless, even in organisations which are not very effective as learning organisations, ways of working and changes can be made at an individual and/or team level to create smaller and more effective learning cultures which can more readily adopt the principles seen above, e.g. sharing learning from practice, which will enable work-based learning to be valued and actively encouraged. These ideas are explored much further in Chapter 5 but the basic necessity of cultivating learning cultures within the workplace underpins all chapters in Section Two of this book.

We can now look at understanding work-based learning as a process in its own right in the next chapter.

FURTHER READING

Gould, N. and Baldwin, M. (2004) *Social Work, Critical Reflection and the Learning Organisation.* Aldershot: Ashgate.

Hafford-Letchfield, T., Leonard, K., Begum, N. and Chick, N. (2008) *Leadership and Management in Social Care.* London: Sage.

SCIE (2004, revised 2008) *Learning Organisations: A self-assessment resource pack.* Available from: www.scie.org.uk/publications

Senge, P. M. (1990) *The Fifth Discipline: The art and practice of a learning organisation.* London: Random House.

Chapter 2
Work-based learning

As seen earlier, professional practice requires working with uncertainty, risk, diversity and difference in a way that recognises oppression, and empowers and promotes the needs and rights of colleagues and fellow workers, as well as users and carers. Adams *et al.* (2009) call this critical practice. Critically reflective practitioners are expected to be self-aware, critically analysing, evaluating, reviewing and updating their values, skills and knowledge, practising flexibly and reflexively, exploring alternative approaches and being open to change in all contexts (Thompson and Thompson, 2008). Critical practice is not about being certain – the certain thing is not necessarily the right thing. It is about being able to deal with uncertainty using sound, valid and accountable processes and, where appropriate, maintain a position of respectful uncertainty, or at least hold on to doubt for longer and seek out other possible versions (Taylor and White, 2006).

Developing capability and competence

As Adams *et al.* (2009) note, being critical means maintaining and representing to others your reasoning and judgement as an independent professional. It involves engagement with, and critical reflection on, experience, which facilitates the promotion of professional values and principles that guide action (Tyreman, 2000: 122). Learning in practice can be understood as change in practice, demonstrating professional capability as well as more basic professional competence.

Competence alone is not enough to equip people to be effective professionals. The demonstration of competence should be seen by anyone enabling learning in the workplace as only part of the overall picture of professional development. Placing too much emphasis on competence-based practice has a number of inherent risks (Doel *et al.*, 2002) as the processes of learning and development can become reduced to tick-box exercises. The danger of this approach is that learning is superficial, with little development of deep understanding of complex issues, or of how skills and knowledge can be transferred from one setting or one problem to another (Biggs, 1999; Barnett and Coate, 2005; Clapton *et al.*, 2006). Success in the workplace is therefore dependent not just on leading and enabling the development of a fixed set of competences but on the development of a range of transferable skills and appropriate professional attributes which interlink to form professional capability (Barnett and Coate, 2005) or dynamic competence (Manor, 2000, cited by Doel *et al.*, 2002).

Barnett and Coate's (2005) holistic model of professional capability is relevant here. It incorporates three interlinked areas, called domains, of knowing, acting and being, which can be understood as notions of knowledge, skills and values. In order to achieve such capability, enablers need to provide practitioners with directed but risk-free opportunities to analyse and evaluate practice critically, explore alternative approaches wherever possible, and develop their own ways to deal effectively with the continuing complexity of practice. The model has clear applicability in work-based learning situations, underlining the importance of your role to maximise opportunities for the development of professional reflexivity, professional self-awareness, the confidence to work independently and take responsibility for one's own practice and one's own professional development.

Skills and attributes that contribute to professional capability include:

- adaptability and reflexivity;

- flexibility and creativity;

- critical analysis and evaluation;

- problem forming and solving;

- team working;

- critical thinking;

- self-reliance and critical self-awareness;

- open-mindedness and recognition of multiple perspectives;

- being able to deal with uncertainty and change;

- motivation to learn and develop, and the ability to learn how to learn.

(Adapted from Williams and Rutter, 2010)

If you can actively enable and encourage learners to incorporate these skills in their practice they will be effective career-long practitioners who can work independently, deal with complexity and embrace change because they will:

- understand the need to keep their knowledge and skills up to date and recognise gaps in their existing capability;

- have the skills and motivation needed to update knowledge and skills independently;

- evaluate new learning and place it in the context of what is already known;

- understand how to adapt and transfer learning from one situation to another, ensuring that they can function effectively when faced with new situations;

- reflect critically on their own practice and the practice of others and use this for the purposes of learning and development;

- be able to articulate and critically evaluate their knowledge to make decision making more systematic;

- be able to use critical thinking skills to solve problems and take responsibility for decision making;

- be able to work effectively with others, recognising and valuing complementary skills and knowledge;

- have professional humility and be open to listening to the views of others;

- have a critical understanding of, and adherence to, an appropriate professional value base.

(Adapted from Barnett and Coate, 2005)

Adult learning principles

Being able to lead and enable such work-based learning also means instilling or fostering a mindset of learning into group work/teams/organisations, as well as establishing or supporting an environment where individuals want to and are able to learn. If the development of the attributes above is seen as crucial to success in social work and other allied professions, then you will need a certain view of learners in the workplace which values them as individuals. This mindset includes working with and maximising the adult learning principles, as developed by Knowles (1980).

Adult learners are autonomous and self-directed

Adults have a different concept of self to children and most adults have reached a point of development where they see themselves as independent and capable of making their own decisions. If they come into a learning situation and have little or no autonomy they may feel disempowered and Knowles believed that this could reduce the quality of their learning.

Adult learners have a wealth of knowledge and experience

Adults approach education with an existing bank of knowledge and experience gained from educational, life and work experiences and this is a resource and foundation for future learning. Knowles believed that adults learn most effectively when they are encouraged to build on and develop their existing knowledge and when they are respected as people who already have skills and knowledge.

Adult learners are goal-oriented

Adults are most motivated to learn things that will help them achieve specific goals. Adults will therefore learn most effectively when the benefits of learning activities are specifically linked to the achievement of learning or life objectives.

Adult learners are relevancy-oriented

Adults are most motivated to learn things they see an immediate use for, particularly learning which will help them 'solve a problem' that they have currently in their lives. Adults will therefore learn most effectively when clear links are made between what they are learning about in theory and how they can use their new knowledge in practice.

Knowles's (1980) claims formed the basis of his theory of andragogy (the study of adult learning) and, although many of his ideas are contentious and are now considered oversimplifications (because many of the characteristics he identified are by no means universal in adults), they are still thought to be a helpful starting point for any discussion about adult learning (Walker *et al.*, 2008). There are some clear implications in his ideas. If we accept his principles as guidance on how to work with adult learners we can see that we will help adults to learn most effectively if we:

- encourage and support them to be active participants in their learning – for example, by setting some or all of their own learning objectives, selecting and designing their own learning experiences and taking some responsibility for monitoring and assessing their own progress and achievements;

- form an adult-to-adult partnership with them that fully takes into account, recognises and values their existing skills and knowledge and uses this as a basis for further learning and development;

- help them to understand how their learning experiences are linked to their learning needs and goals.

ACTIVITY *2.1*

Adult learning principles

Reflect on Knowles's principles for adult learning and consider how well they describe you as a learner. For example, do you always learn most effectively when you are able to be in control of your own learning or can you think of times when you would prefer to be more directed?

This exercise will help you to begin to think about some of the reasons why Knowles's theory of andragogy (1980) is controversial. Most people find that the extent to which they want to manage their own learning varies from situation to situation and will be dependent on a number of complex interacting variables such as confidence levels, context, learning task and time pressures. Every adult learner and every learning situation is unique.

Encouraging practitioners to take an active responsibility for their own learning and to be meaningfully involved in the process is important and can enhance their learning outcomes (Knowles, 1980, 1990). However, not everyone will be in the secure and confident position necessary to be able to accept this responsibility. Also, people in new situations or who are being asked to make frequent and/or fundamental changes to their practice often feel anxious, destabilised and disoriented. This is a fundamental element in the learning process, especially when change and relearning are involved (Atherton, 2011a); it needs to be planned for and managed in a way which respects and fully supports those involved, rather than seeing them as obstructive or just difficult. If someone is resistant to learning there is usually a genuine underlying reason. Indeed, any number of personal issues may be creating undue stress and impacting on professional life, and someone's routines and established practice may become that person's anchor points. Any change in practice can then involve transformative learning (see Chapter 6), and this will be dealt with more effectively in an open dialogue where the person is given the same kind of respect and care as that extended to service users and/or patients.

Informal learning: using experience and reflection

Although formal opportunities for learning have an important role in professional development, they are by no means the only ways that professionals learn. In the workplace learning is happening pretty much all of the time. Whenever something new is encountered there is the potential to learn from it – even familiar situations offer opportunities for further developing knowledge and skills if they are approached in a certain way. Informal methods include ad hoc conversations with colleagues in the office or in the car, learning through practice experience, learning from discussions with service users, observing or working alongside colleagues, attendance at meetings and visits to other agencies. When we are talking to people we can enable them to be more analytical and critical in their thinking. This may help them to learn more from their experiences, and encouraging learning to be shared with others can help teams to learn and develop more effectively.

Informal learning has some strengths because it can expose people to a wide variety of approaches and ideas and can be a very efficient and relevant way to learn. However, it can also pass on poor practice through habit or the adoption of uncritical approaches and ideas, and so there is a need to be aware that informal learning can sometimes be incomplete or partially understood and requires critical appraisal. Recognising the need to make the most of informal as well as more formal learning to develop practice becomes a critical habit of mind (Rutter and Brown, 2011). Informal learning events like observation, feedback, dialogue, and co-working usually result in new knowing or understanding that is either tacit or regarded as part of a person's general capability, rather than as something 'learnt'. However, it is a key area for professional development. To make any learning more explicit and meaningful requires a commitment to approaching it systematically and with a questioning stance, i.e. planning for it, recording it, critically reflecting on it, actively using the ideas in practice and evaluating the outcomes.

Key models for experiential and reflective learning identify important stages or aspects of this learning that need to be planned for or managed when leading and enabling others in the workplace.

In Kolb's (1984) *experiential learning model*, the process of learning is described as a staged, cyclical model involving the four learning modes which may be entered at any stage, and the cycle perpetuates itself. Concrete experience is followed by reflection on that experience, which is then followed by the consideration of general ideas and concepts describing the experience, or the linking of known theories to it (abstract conceptualisation), and hence to the planning of the next occurrence of the experience (active experimentation), leading in turn to the next concrete experience. Learning therefore takes place in a cycle and you would plan for each stage to be a specific part of the learning experience. You could also enable the learner to undertake various processes within each of the stages to maximise the learning, e.g. designing the learning experience in the first place, encouraging use of reflective models and questioning techniques for the reflective phase, encouraging theory-to-practice links for the analytical phase and then promoting the use of action plans for the next phase.

Kolb's (1984) model is criticised for being a rather technical, staged approach (Miettinen, 2000; Coffield *et al.*, 2004) and does not take into account the more emotional aspects of learning. In contrast, Race's (2010) *ripples model*, although less theoretical, does include these aspects and his elements interact with one another like ripples in a pond, creating an integrated, interacting whole that constitutes successful learning.

The elements are:

- *wanting*: the motivation for learning – this is the internal circle;

- *feedback*: seeing the results, other people's reactions – this is the external circle;

- *doing*: the practice, or trial and error, and *digesting*, making sense of it, reflecting on it, gaining ownership – these are the internal overlapping processes or circles which interact with each other and which are continuously influenced both by internally generated needing/wanting and by externally generated feedback.

By working with this model any learning opportunity will be driven by the learner's motivation so that the 'doing', the opportunities for 'digesting' or reflecting and 'feedback' are all positively engaged with. Here, you could consider how your role may be slightly different than if you were following Kolb's model as you may be considering the design of the learning task from a much more motivational angle.

Both models include a reflective element. Reflection allows the most significant learning to be drawn out from any experience because it helps to lift subconscious or informal learning to a more conscious and formalised level, using critically analytical questions (e.g. how? how else? why? why else?) and evaluative questions (e.g. how well? how better?). Only such conscious learning and development becomes educative in a true sense (i.e. deep, meaningful and owned), and thus able to impact on the development of professional judgement and expertise, and in turn to enhance service quality.

For Boud *et al.* (1985: 19) reflection is an activity in which people *recapture their experience, think about it, mull it over and evaluate it.* They focus on the key aspects of returning to an experience, attending to or connecting with feelings, evaluating the experience and integrating the new knowledge. It is a process that involves, amongst other things, the consideration of self and one's own experiences of practice (Doel *et al.,* 2002).

There are many ways people reflect and, indeed, it is a very individual activity, rather like learning. There also seem to be a range of different possible outcomes. We would not like to prescribe any one method over any other, but there are a few principles relating to the nature of reflection to take note of. It should:

- lead to learning and be committed to action;

- be holistic by encouraging the integration of learning across all three required areas for professional capability – a learner's knowing, acting and being;

- be developmental;

- be critical, i.e. it is not just skills or knowledge that are 'reviewed', rather a new view of practice is achieved as the assumptions or 'givens' associated with certain methods or practices are also scrutinised.

(Adapted from Williams and Rutter, 2010)

In order to achieve this, any enabling of reflection means that the leader/enabler should ensure the conditions for it are right and that certain features are apparent:

- emotionally supportive – feeling safe, respected, valued;

- appropriate levels of challenge – unsettling but not threatening;

- allow active listening;

- suspension of your own frame of reference and judgements;

- consideration of other perspectives and approaches and an acceptance that there is no single 'truth';

- framework of critical questions – asking why and why again;

- an understanding that change may not always occur – the process can sometimes lead to affirmation of practice and be strengths-based in developing expertise.

The informal and ongoing nature of work-based learning can be seen as important aspects when developing practice and aiming to enhance one's career. This can now be explored further in the following chapter, which looks at continuing professional development.

FURTHER READING

Beverley, A. and Worsley, A. (2007) *Learning and Teaching in Social Work Practice.* London: Palgrave Macmillan.

Fraser, S. and Matthews, S. (2008) *The Critical Practitioner in Social Work and Health Care.* London: Sage.

Parker, J. (2010) *Effective Practice Learning in Social Work* (2nd edn). Exeter: Learning Matters.

Chapter 3
Continuing professional development (CPD)

CPD is *the learning in which professionals engage in the context of their working lives* (O'Sullivan, 2006: 1). It involves the maintenance and enhancement of knowledge, expertise and competence throughout a career, meeting the needs of the professional, the employer, the profession and society itself. Its purpose is to enhance the quality of practice and therefore service quality too. Munro (2011: 116) states that it is essential for professionals to *engage productively* in CPD, supporting both formal and informal methods, i.e. systematic training or education as well as work-based activities.

The importance of continually developing, and being able to demonstrate, CPD is an essential prerequisite set by the Health and Care Professions Council (HCPC), the successors to the General Social Care Council (GSCC) as the new body for professional social work registration. However, at the time of writing, neither the content nor amount of CPD undertaken is specified within the HPC requirements (although there is an emphasis on the impact CPD activities have on practice). In social work a new national CPD framework (**www.collegeofsocialwork.org**) is also encouraging the articulation and assessment of learning and development occurring within educational and practice settings.

Learning objectives

CPD usually involves four stages in an ongoing cycle (Figure 3.1).

The key points are:

- The individual is responsible for managing and undertaking his/her CPD activity.

- The process needs to be planned (although, of course, learning sometimes happens in very unplanned ways).

- Learning objectives are essential and should serve organisational as well as individual goals and/or needs.

Individual practitioners will need to demonstrate what impact CPD has had on their practice, but any measurement or assessment of this will be a challenge without clear and agreed learning agreements or objectives, which is why they are a key element here. Enabling and leading others to identify and/or develop those learning objectives becomes an important role for any enabler of learning in the workplace. Of course, informal learning is important here and almost by definition isn't planned, which means that learning and indeed learning needs can

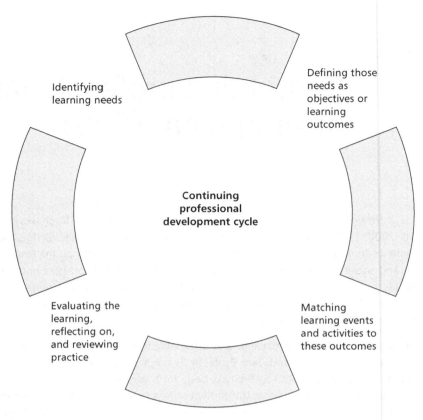

Identifying learning needs

Defining those needs as objectives or learning outcomes

Continuing professional development cycle

Evaluating the learning, reflecting on, and reviewing practice

Matching learning events and activities to these outcomes

Figure 3.1 Continuing professional development cycle. © Ivan Gray.

emerge from action rather than being initially identified and planned for. The CPD process can be a very managed or managerial approach that sometimes doesn't do justice to the complexity of working life. The person enabling CPD can take this into account by encouraging reflection that can help identify impromptu learning and/or emergent learning needs.

Attitudes to CPD

Although sometimes onerous, undertaking CPD is the mark of good professional practice, but there is an additional important point to be made. Cooper (2008: 222) argues that *the attitudes of professional workers to their CPD is a strong indicator, if not a defining feature, of their approach to practice*. There is a fundamental link in how CPD is viewed and its impact on practitioners – it is about the quality of their working lives. If it is viewed by workers as something done to them it will probably be seen as an additional burden on top of the 'real' work they are doing. Any involvement in it is likely to be superficial and also resented. If, instead, it is seen as part of a professional or work-based role and owned, it is likely to be much more meaningful and relevant to their work, and have a positive impact on practice, and on them as people in a more general sense. We can see that working to adult learning principles when leading and enabling learning can help you achieve this as you encourage and model a more active and responsible stance towards CPD.

There is another aspect to be aware of with regard to how knowledge or skills are actually viewed. They can be seen as things that essentially have to stay the same, i.e. they cannot be criticised, interpreted or changed in any way. You may know of educators who only show students how to do things their way, or practitioners who stick to one theoretical model or who are entrenched in particular ways of working. Alternatively, knowledge and skills can be seen in a more active and flexible way, as things to be criticised, interpreted or changed as they are used and developed in new situations and by different people. Adams *et al.* (2009) agree and argue that developing professional expertise is about building knowledge in and for different situations – they call it contextual knowledge development. They say that expertise:

> *is learnt in context but what is developed is knowledge which allows this learning to be applied successfully in new and diverse situations.*

(Adams *et al.*, 2009: 240)

In other words, the understanding and wisdom that we develop in specific practice situations can be used in a range of other situations because we are constantly developing and adapting it. This way of looking at knowledge (i.e. critically constructing valid meaning for yourself and being able to develop a confident 'knowing' for different situations) aligns well with the critical, questioning and open stance needed for professional capability, work-based learning and CPD. This approach is more able to take account of uncertain and complex situations; it requires self-motivated and reflective learners engaged holistically in self-directed, ongoing and evaluated learning.

CPD will expect you, and the people you are leading and enabling, to interpret, adapt and evaluate knowledge and skills in use and produce ideas of your/their own as a result. We all have the right and also the responsibility as professionals to reason through and evaluate knowledge or methods in respect of how well they 'perform' in practice situations and in respect of our values, and then articulate the results as new understanding and valid knowledge.

ACTIVITY **3.1**

Your learning and CPD

Think about the ideas being presented here. Do they match your own ideas about learning and knowledge?

Write a statement that describes the notion of CPD for you.

Independent learning and self-leadership

The notions of self-leadership and independent learning are very relevant here. Hock (2000) states that the first and paramount responsibility of anyone who purports to manage is to manage self, and so this aspect of taking responsibility for our own professional development is pivotal. It is about taking responsibility for learning and development rather than relying on organisations to drive this. It involves everyone in their own curriculum planning, i.e. designing the structure and content of what is learnt and the process of learning itself. Independent learning and self-leadership are about seeing learning as something everyone actively takes part in and helps design; it cannot be viewed in a traditional manner of expecting a teacher to provide a complete package of aims and content (i.e. the specific outcomes, all the materials, ideas and routes) and the pupils just to receive them and then replicate them somehow.

For leaders and managers, the aim is to ensure that practitioners are fully enabled and prepared to achieve this. As we saw earlier, not all adult learners are ready or able to take an active role in their learning and it is essential to work with people to explore this further in a nurturing rather than controlling way, and to help build the necessary skills for effective CPD. If we use these ideas and the CPD cycle above we can see these skills involve:

- taking the initiative in diagnosing learning needs;

- creating learning objectives (rather than identifying training courses to go on);

- identifying, locating and evaluating the resources/training/education needed;

- choosing and implementing appropriate learning strategies and mobilising a range of learning methods to respond to needs;

- keeping CPD under regular review in supervision;

- evaluating learning outcomes;

- evaluating CPD also in terms of improved outcomes for people who use services.

The active development of these skills in others can help CPD to become a fully supported and systematic process for individual but also organisational learning.

FURTHER READING

Cooper, B. (2008) Continuing professional development: a critical approach. In: Fraser, S. and Matthews, S. (eds) *The Critical Practitioner in Social Work and Health Care*. London: Sage: 222–237.

Fook, J., Ryan, M. and Hawkins, L. (2000) *Professional Expertise: Practice, theory and education for working in uncertainty*. London: Whiting and Birch.

Rutter, L. (2012) *Continuing Professional Development in Social Work*. London: Sage.

Thompson, N. (2006) *Promoting Workplace Learning*. Bristol: Policy Press.

Chapter 4
Review: skills and attributes

Although everyone has the innate capacity and potential to learn from any situation in which they find themselves, learning or development often does not take place. A number of factors impact on the learning of individuals within the workplace, some of which relate to the situation or environment in which they function and others relate more directly to the ability of the person at that time to make sense of and apply the new information that the individual is receiving.

You can effectively model, lead and enable a deeper, more meaningful approach to work-based learning and development by understanding and using the ideas associated with learning organisations and cultures, professional competence and capability, adult learning principles, experiential and reflective learning and continuing professional development. This philosophy of learning can underpin your work on a macro as well as a micro scale, i.e. whether you are developing a communication system within an entire organisation, a team-based learning culture or a one-to-one partnership with someone.

What you bring to this process (in respect of your attributes, attitude, beliefs and under-standing of managing, leading and enabling, and learning) is also important to consider. It is not necessarily what managers and leaders do but rather the way it is done which can have the most significant impact on others.

ACTIVITY **4.1**

Existing skills for the role

Write a few words on the skills, knowledge and personal qualities you are bringing to the role of leader or enabler of others.

Remember that skills and knowledge are often transferable from other areas of your life. For instance, you may never have had experience of leading or enabling adults to learn in a formal setting but you may know that you are good at engaging with patients or service users. Think about how you will need to build on these skills, knowledge and attributes as you become more experienced within the role. What new knowledge will you need? What skills will you need to develop? Where will values fit in?

This exercise will provide you with an analysis of your existing skills, knowledge and values and will encourage you to think about areas for further development. This could form the basis for an action plan for your own continuing professional development.

We would maintain that working to adult learning principles means adopting a leadership or management style that works *with* others and their strengths in order to lead and enable learning and development. As a philosophical approach to organisational effectiveness, leadership emphasises the need to inspire and motivate staff, as individuals or as groups, rather than push and drive them using controls and sanctions.

The need for humility as well as honesty within a critically reflective stance is a key point here too. It especially holds true when you are working in a partnership of trust with other staff. You have to model reflective behaviour in order to be credible but the extra awareness that humility can bring to the process may help address some of the power issues between managers/leaders and others; it may enhance sensitivity towards another person's perspective and allow a more productive stance of working in partnership with that person. Recent theory (Lawlor and Bilson, 2010) has also highlighted the importance of managerial and leadership approaches that are appropriate to the ethical and moral nature of social work practice, i.e. those that take account of personal and interpersonal elements of the role. Leading and enabling the learning of others requires enthusiasm, adaptability, innovation and courage, but perhaps, overall, an ability to adopt a person-centred approach.

Section 2

Chapter 5
Communities
of practice

Engagement in social practice is the fundamental process through which we learn and become who we are.

(Wenger, 1998)

In Section One we established the importance of learning that moves beyond the individual and impacts on the way that organisations and, indeed, groups of organisations function. In this chapter we will look at how social learning supports and enhances opportunities for individuals to learn and provides an effective vehicle for improving wider learning and communication within and across organisational boundaries.

By exploring and evaluating a form of social learning – a community of practice (Lave and Wenger, 1991) – we will consider your role as a manager or leader in enabling professionals to learn through engagement with others who have shared interests and/or common experiences. This could be through involvement in setting up a new community of practice to meet an identified learning need or by improving the way that an existing community functions. Although social learning happens naturally in most organisations, modern working practices can act as barriers to the process. Before we move on to look at some of the key ideas and methods that you can adopt to enable learning through communities of practice, it may be helpful for you to take a few moments to reflect on your work environment and the impact that the following may have on your organisation's capacity to enable social learning to occur.

- The culture for learning within the organisation. Note: managerialist, top-down and risk-averse cultures tend to stifle critical reflection, limit engagement from workers with creativity and block learning (Beddoe, 2009).

- Opportunities to meet people with shared interests and experiences within own organisation. Note: increased home working, shift working and high caseloads are decreasing regular face-to-face contact between workers in some organisations.

- Opportunities to meet people with shared interests and experiences outside own organisation. Note: budget constraints and restrictions on travel in some organisations are reducing opportunities for wider networking.

- The focus and style of contact between individuals – is there a forum for open discussion, critical analysis and evaluation, or are all meetings task- and target-oriented?

- The learning skills, motivation and openness to learning of individual workers.

- The support given by managers and supervisors to value, embed and reinforce learning achieved (Gray *et al.*, 2010a).

- The use of internet-based technology to connect people virtually to supplement, augment or replace face-to-face contact.

Why is social learning important?

If you think back to your first professional job you will be able to list several ways in which you learnt what you were expected to do. An important source of learning was almost certainly the people in your team and a great deal of your initial professional development was probably supported by observation and discussion with colleagues. Although this form of social learning is particularly important in the early stages of our working lives, it continues to be a significant influence at all stages of our careers. In 1991, Lave and Wenger used the term 'community of practice' to explain how social (or situated) learning can occur within a work arena when people come together.

Lave and Wenger's ideas on communities of practice were based on social learning theories (e.g. Vygotsky, 1986) which provided new ways of understanding how people learn. Rather than thinking of knowledge as a fixed entity that could be transferred from one individual to another, social learning theories were based on the premise that knowledge is socially constructed. In other words, what we know is not fixed and certain, but evolves over time and is influenced by the experiences that we have along the way. Exposure to new ideas, experiences and different perspectives changes the way we think and the inherent beliefs of the communities in which we live and work influence our understanding and our values. Lave and Wenger used these ideas to explain why learning from other members of a professional community is such a fundamental part of individual growth. They believed that their model could help people to understand how and why learning takes place and how professional knowledge and capability develop over time. Their work helps us to appreciate just how important it is to provide appropriate social learning opportunities to support the development of social workers' professional capability and also to strengthen the knowledge and skills base of the organisations that employ them.

What is a community of practice?

Most of us already belong to a number of communities of practice – usually without knowing that we do so! This is because many communities of practice are not explicitly labelled as such and are either informal and naturally occurring, or part of an existing structure such as a team or professional grouping.

According to Wenger *et al.* (2002), communities of practice are formed by people who are engaged in the process of collective learning in a shared domain of human endeavour.

To be defined as a community of practice the members must:

- have a shared interest or domain;

- interact purposefully together as a community, helping each other and sharing information;

- use their involvement to improve their practice.

Using the above definition you will be able to identify some meetings and other points of contact between individuals in your organisation that could be functioning as communities of practice. Although we don't normally think of routine meetings and everyday contacts in terms of the learning that can be achieved, it could be argued that they all should be constructed not only to achieve service outcomes but also to maximise opportunities for social learning to occur. Unfortunately, social work's dominant managerial culture tends to force us to think about meetings primarily as places to pass on information and get tasks done. Although these 'business objectives' will justifiably remain a priority in the majority of meetings we attend, focusing some of our attention on the way that people in groups learn together will help us to create a culture for learning and improve the overall quality of the learning that takes place.

Communities of practice offer rich learning opportunities and members can benefit in a number of ways, such as:

- support with problem solving;

- opportunities to discuss approaches to practice;

- opportunities to discuss and evaluate new developments;

- information exchange (top-down, bottom-up and side-to-side);

- recycling and sharing of assets;

- co-ordination and synergy;

- mapping of knowledge and gaps in knowledge;

- opportunities to observe other practitioners or other organisations with a similar role or purpose.

Communities can be large or small, confined within organisational boundaries or extended beyond them. As we have already seen, they are not necessarily groups deliberately convened for structured learning (their stated function could be, for example, networking or information exchange or management); they don't need to be formally constituted, have a fixed membership or even meet face to face. For example, a multi-professional group from a mental health team who meet weekly for a case review meeting or a group of colleagues from different children and families teams who meet informally for coffee quarterly to discuss developments in their field, or even the members of a team who meet up at the end of a day to debrief and share experiences could all be considered to be communities of practice. A group of practice educators who participate in an internet-based chat room to exchange hints and tips about working with students or a monthly drop-in journal club at which workers can share interesting new pieces of research would also meet the definition. Although many communities of practice are naturally occurring with a fluid membership and evolving concerns and remits, others can be more actively set up and managed, e.g. a team meeting, a regional practice educators forum, a monthly interprofessional case review group or an internet-based national community of practice for public sector workers.

As we think about what could be defined as a community of practice we can see that in most workplaces there are multiple opportunities for people to meet with others and learn from the experience. However, we need to question whether all situations in which people work together in groups are functioning as communities of practice and indeed whether appropriate social learning is always an outcome of this type of group membership. Think back to the last team meeting that you attended. What agenda items were covered and what was the nature of the discussion that took place? How much time was spent in open discussion and critical reflection? How did the dynamics and relationships between people in the team impact on the engagement of team members in the discussion and the extent to which individual voices were heard?

Work teams and project groups that are primarily brought together to give and receive information or to get a job done using predetermined strategies and goals may not be functioning as communities of practice. Communication in such groups may be almost exclusively top-down and individual members may feel disempowered and left without a voice. Opportunities for social learning are limited when there is no scope for members to share their experiences and develop their ideas through discussion and debate. At this point it may be worth reflecting on the way that meetings are structured in your organisation and considering whether aspects of those meetings could be developed to support more opportunities for learning and development for both individual participants and the organisation as a whole (e.g. by including more interactive agenda items, slots for people to talk about new ideas and initiatives and by supporting all members to participate in discussions and decision making).

What are the advantages of taking a 'communities of practice' approach to learning and development?

In the business world, communities of practice are often seen as ways of increasing productivity by capturing and sharing tacit knowledge and increasing responsiveness to market demands (Wenger *et al.*, 2002). Although in social work we use a different language, effective communities of practice can help organisations achieve similar objectives by enabling them to respond quickly to change. They do this by shortening 'learning curves' for individual workers through the sharing of knowledge and experience. They can also improve communication across and between organisations and increase employees' engagement, motivation and job satisfaction. Because communities of practice foster an open approach to new ideas, they provide increased opportunities for the voice of service users and carers to be heard and for messages about their needs and wishes to be communicated more widely (Gray *et al.*, 2010a). Finally, because there is a focus on critical learning in communities of practice, they provide excellent scaffolding for the development of professional capability, peer learning and networking – seen by the Social Work Reform Board as essential elements of a comprehensive continuing professional development framework (SWRB, 2010).

How do communities of practice arise?

As we have already seen, some communities of practice can be by-products of structures set up for other purposes. Team meetings are a good example of this. Although learning is not the primary purpose of this type of forum, good leadership can support the creation of a culture in which opportunities for social learning are maximised. Other communities of practice arise because individuals or groups recognise that benefits will be gained from linking with other people. Sometimes this recognition will lead to formal efforts being made to establish a community (which may even be labelled as a community of practice) but more often groupings evolve naturally as the need to learn together arises.

Wenger *et al.* (2002) believe that it is wrong to think in terms of purposefully creating a community of practice; they suggest that a community of practice exists naturally wherever there is a task that involves more than one person. However, these authors acknowledge that the existence of a community per se does not ensure that it provides an effective environment for learning and development – links between individuals can be weak and factors may be in operation, such as individualistic cultures and unequal power, that prevent co-operation and information sharing (Beddoe, 2009). Addressing this issue, Plaskoff (2006) suggests that community-building activities are critical if the potential for communities of practice to support learning within organisations is to be realised. He identified a number of factors which were fundamental to the successful operation of a community of practice, including trust, a sense of belonging, equality and thriving relationships between group members. He pointed out that in traditional hierarchical organisations trust can be undermined by the way that power is distributed and community building blocked by a lack of commitment to joint working. This is supported by a study by Beddoe (2009) which highlighted the fact that practitioners felt that cultures within social care organisations did not support learning effectively. As with learning organisations, communities of practice seem to require new approaches to management and leadership, with democratic and distributed approaches to leadership fitting most appropriately.

What does community building mean?

So, if the simple act of bringing people together does not necessarily result in a successful community of practice, how can a group of people be turned into a community in which learning thrives? Like Plaskoff, Wenger (2006) recognises the importance of community building and suggests an approach which includes the following features.

- Education – helping people understand why communities of practice are important to their work and how they can contribute.

- Support – providing 'light-touch' support to the community, e.g. IT facilities, co-ordination (but not management of the community).

- Action – getting going as soon as possible because people will be encouraged by seeing communities in action.

- Encouragement – publicising success, encouraging developments and identifying sponsors who will promote the value of involvement.

- Integration – bringing the work of the communities of practice into the organisation, preventing them from feeling marginalised and irrelevant to the development of the organisation as a whole.

Wenger suggests that a core group of people can be gathered to start the community-building process and take early responsibility for increasing involvement in the group. As a manager you could decide to take the lead in this process, or you could enable and support someone else to take a leadership role. We have already established that communities of practice function most effectively when members have equal status. So, if you wanted to foster the development of a community of practice in your workplace, you would need to think carefully about the approach that you take to community building. This will include thinking about what leadership style you would adopt and how much direct responsibility you should directly take for the process of setting up and co-ordinating the group.

Plaskoff (2006) puts forward a model for community building which has many similarities to Wenger's approach, but in which he suggests that a more managed approach is needed to increase the chances of success. He suggests starting with a small development team with a remit to agree philosophical underpinnings, development processes and common under-standings. This group then works with a subset of the whole community to set priorities before involving others. Working within the Plaskoff model gives the option for managers to provide impetus and work as part of the development team whilst still adopting distributed approach to leadership within the process (Gray *et al.*, 2010a).

How can communities of practice be sustained?

Getting a community of practice started is perhaps a small challenge compared to sustaining interest and enthusiasm in the longer term. A research study by Beddoe (2009) uncovered a strong commitment to the principles of learning amongst social workers. However, in the current climate – with social workers reporting ever-increasing pressures on their time – it is questionable whether genuine engagement in activities that are perceived to be primarily about learning will be prioritised over meeting day-to-day targets. The author's own experience of mentor groups for new practice educators justifies this concern and points to the importance of taking a pragmatic approach, wherever possible embedding or linking communities of practice to existing frameworks and resources. Even when workers are given permission to be involved in learning activities, the overall target-driven culture that they work within will often mean that they opt to give low priority to anything seen as not directly linked to the provision of service. But, as we have seen in this chapter, learning does not have to be about attending expensive (in time as well as money) training courses but can result from practice experience itself. Small changes in the way that people work together to encourage and enable them to share ideas and experiences can provide an efficient and cost-effective way of reducing 'silo' working and improving both individual and organisational learning in the workplace.

The following have been identified as key factors in sustaining commitment within a community of practice:

- being explicit about the benefits of the community by publicising advantages people have gained from participation to people inside and outside the group;

- allowing the community to evolve naturally to meet the needs of members;

- creating opportunities for open dialogue and supporting this by bringing in people who can provide other perspectives to the group (service users, carers and other professionals);

- allowing different levels of participation – it should not be compulsory to attend and people should not be pushed into contributing (this may not be possible in some forms of community of practice, e.g. teams);

- getting a balance between more routine information-exchange types of activities and more exciting brainstorming and thinking outside the box;

- finding the right rhythm and routine with the group meeting often enough to sustain commitment but not too often;

- allowing space for members to talk privately and not just within the whole group.

(Adapted from Wenger *et al.*, 2002)

Beddoe, L. (2009) Creating continuous conversation: social workers and learning organisations. *Social Work Education*, 28(7): 722–736.

Gray, I., Parker, J., Rutter, L. and Williams, S. (2010) Developing communities of practice: effective leadership, management and supervision in social work. *Social Sciences Review,* 14(2): 20–36.

Plaskoff, J. (2006) Intersubjectivity and community building: learning to learn organisationally. In: Easterby-Smith, M. and Lyles, M.A. (eds) *Handbook of Organisational Learning and Knowledge Management.* Oxford: Blackwell.

See also Etienne Wenger's website (**http://wenger-trayner.com/**) for good examples of communities of practice and information on community building.

Chapter 6
Change management

In this chapter we will consider the type of learning that is happening during periods of organisational change and the most appropriate ways to try and enable that learning. Organisational change might be considered to have a managerial focus but it can be seen that change, leading and learning are interrelated. Hafford-Letchfield *et al.* (2008) show that learning is very much linked to change management and therefore people who understand how to facilitate learning can make an important contribution to the change process.

> *Leadership is closely connected with the concept of change, and change, in turn, is at the essence of the learning process.*
>
> (Brown and Pozner, 2001: 275–276)

Leaders are actually often called change agents. Therefore, those who can learn effectively in a range of situations should be able to create the conditions in which others can learn and develop, and engage positively with the necessary and ongoing changes in an organisational learning culture. In effect, anyone can lead and enable change; it does not have to be a manager or someone in a leadership role. In many respects it may be better if it isn't, as enabling change is not just about leading and managing the change itself – it is about understanding and enabling other people during change, or even just bringing in some new ideas to the team. These thoughts are explored further below.

Types of change

One important factor is that the constant impact of strategic policies and other requirements on organisations now mean that change is inevitable, continual and affects most aspects of our working lives, e.g. resource allocation, systems and procedures.

There are different types of change, although most try to improve performance or output in one way or another:

- process change – the set of activities which are used to generate the outputs of an organisation, e.g. new assessment forms;

- system change – sets of procedures, e.g. detaining someone under the Mental Health Act;

- structural change – the outward form of an organisation, e.g. hierarchies, new departments, fewer middle managers;

- organisational-level change – relates to inherent culture and identity, e.g. change of purpose for a department or an organisation; being driven by new government-imposed targets.

Changes may be:

- incremental (i.e. doing things better);

- transitional (i.e. new strategies);

- transformational (i.e. comprehensive change at several levels).

(Mabey, 2001: 9)

Therefore, the way we view change should acknowledge and work with this condition of constant change as a given, rather than something that happens intermittently. Most authors call for creativity, flexibility, adaptability and responsiveness in order to deal with this notion and create a readiness for change. However, it is also acknowledged that working to these high levels of capability takes a toll on people's ability to perform in their roles, especially when so much change is inevitably seen, or proves to be change for change's sake.

Strategies: 'hard' issues

Strategies for leading change usually focus on the hard issues – tasks, procedures, roles and outcomes (i.e. people's behaviours, skills and actions). These strategies encompass areas of project and change management, e.g. Kotter (1996) provides a management model with an eight-step cycle.

In general terms change management includes:

1. a clear, unified sense of direction and vision;

2. planning and foresight;

3. realistic goals and achievable solutions;

4. clear ownership and leadership;

5. workable plans;

6. prioritised details;

7. decisions made on what to do first;

8. changes measured and monitored.

Strategies: 'soft' issues

An alternative change strategy looks at more fundamental and intrinsic change, i.e. changing people's mindsets, their ways of being and relating. Here, organisational change strategies are better aligned to the affective and relational nature of health and social service (i.e. the emotions and personal/interpersonal aspects). Because change needs to be achieved with, for, and through people, it requires sound understanding and skills in working with and enabling others. The one thing that will always make change happen in the wrong way is the lack of involvement and communication with those affected by the change. These may be called the 'soft issues' but they are absolutely pivotal to the success of any change. As we have seen, leading and enabling others is about what you do and how you do it. The same principle is at work here – it is not so much what change is being implemented but rather how it is done that makes the difference between a good or bad experience.

ACTIVITY 6.1

Organisations handling change

Can you list some negative and positive ways in which change has been handled in an organisation in which you have worked? What was the impact on staff?

Leading and enabling change

There are two key areas for concern when talking about the people involved in or affected by the processes of change:

1. their perceptions and attitudes to the change;

2. additional training and support requirements.

Firstly, perception and attitude are everything. Whilst logic and reasons for change may be clear in business or service delivery terms, not every individual will see it that way. This is why communication is absolutely essential here; lack of participation or sharing of information creates a 'lose–lose' situation because it engenders a lack of trust and feelings of powerlessness in people. If there is confusion or resentment about the change then it is obvious that people will not be in the best frame of mind to work or learn. Research (Chrusciel and Field, 2006) shows that perception of personal gain is also important here, i.e. a person's aspirations and individual personal goals. People not only need to be engaged in the change process, but they also need to benefit from it. This is not about a selfish 'what's in it for me' attitude, rather creating a means for 'buy-in' based on the perception of meaningful change and fulfilling professional values. These are relevant and important social learning features. As noted above, perception and attitude are everything and, if the processes and methods of change are impartial, inclusive and productive for all, they should be seen positively.

However, 'winning hearts and minds' is only part of the story. Staff also need to be able to undertake any new tasks or fulfil new roles effectively. Resources, skills, knowledge and values need to be reviewed in respect of the changes and any shortfalls or gaps identified early on and appropriate support/training/education built into the process. The changes may require more fundamental development too – a shift in priorities or values. Learning concerns not only areas of competency but also more advanced capability (Williams and Rutter, 2010).

Leading the learning for change

Another way to look at strategies for change takes account of the people-centred skills and attributes that can allow learning to take its central place in the process of leading change. The idea of being learner-centred, seen earlier in Section One, is very relevant here and reiterated within the key principles below.

- Recognise that you are a role model.

- Be visible, and listen to concerns – encourage constructive debate and feedback.

- Even if you do not buy in fully to what is happening yourself, you still have a responsibility to help others through the process in a supportive, positive and constructive way.

- Be consistent in what you say, and never speculate – if you do not know or cannot say, then say so.

- Be empathetic to concerns, and help people understand what is *actually* happening, not what they *think* is happening.

- Go out of your way to involve people and explain what is happening.

- Let people get involved in the details about what needs to be changed.

- Provide open explanation about why certain decisions are being made.

- Focus on, understand and meet team-working and team development needs.

- Define the specific attributes, actions and interactions needed from individuals.

(Adapted from Robert Gordon University, c. 2008)

Individuals and change

We can now take a deeper look at how individuals cope with the type of learning that comes with change. For many learners there will be a personal cost in letting go of something in order to take on board something new. This personal cost is associated with a 'supplantive learning' view, as explained by Atherton (2011a), and a number of his ideas are explored here. As he says, up until this point a member of staff, e.g. Pete, may have been getting along quite nicely, thank you, with tried and familiar forms of practice and beliefs, until someone comes along and tells him that what he has been doing and believing is now wrong in some way or needs to be changed. It is therefore not surprising if Pete's initial inclination is to reject the new material and carry on in his usual way.

Supplantive learning can therefore entail a degree of loss of competence, and perhaps of confidence, because a previous skill (or item of knowledge) has to be abandoned or rejected while the learner is still on the learning curve with the new understanding or skill. This loss of competence can cause a large amount of frustration and despondency, sufficient for the person to abandon the learning/change process. Problematic supplantive learning seems most likely to occur when there is a considerable emotional investment in the old methods of learning, usually related to personal history or the concept of self. For example, Pete might say, 'You mean I've been doing it wrong all these years?' or 'I've always thought of myself as a good social worker'.

Represented graphically, the curve of the old learning and that of the new learning produce a 'learning trough' (Figure 6.1).

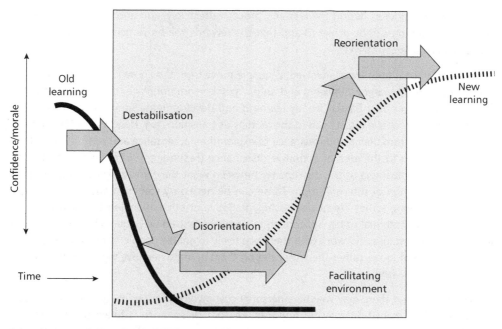

Figure 6.1 Supplantive learning (Atherton, 2011a).

As Atherton explains, the initial destabilisation stage has two components – the declaration of the change and the potential learner's, i.e. Pete's, application of it to him- or herself. The learning process can only begin when a direction for the change has been declared.

The next stage, disorientation, corresponds to Pete's journey across the landscape where he is letting go of old learning but only just starting to grasp or engage with the new material. He therefore has little to hold on to or feel confident about. Disorientation can be readily recognised and described, as it often engages strong feelings such as depression, anger, exhaustion and frustration, even guilt. There may also be moments of excitement and a sense of liberation from the past, but these are usually short-lived. There may also be 'attempts at apathy' in which the whole learning enterprise is dismissed; either these become permanent, in which case the learning process is abandoned, or they fail to last. The specific emotional pattern, of course, varies from individual to individual. Atherton (2011a) explains that it can bear a distinct and not unexpected resemblance to the pattern of grief.

The final stage of reorientation is where Pete is faced with integrating the new learning into his overall belief system or conduct, and has eventually to face the challenges posed by such learning in the real world. This can be difficult, and, as Atherton (2011a) says, there is some evidence that difficulties encountered in practice can reawaken the losses experienced in the earlier disorientation phase, so that the trough as described here repeats itself *like a diminishing echo as the new learning becomes established.*

As you can see from Figure 6.1, the facilitating environment is vital to making the whole experience more positive as it provides the conditions under which growth and learning can potentially take place – safety, understanding and trust. It is the role of the enabler to manage the feelings engendered during the learning process effectively, and encourage the learner to believe that learning can be achieved and that the rewards will be sufficient to counteract the difficulties being encountered.

This is an emotional time for all involved as people move from the known to the unknown, and feelings of being threatened, anxiety and anger may be commonplace. It seems obvious that these emotions can be a barrier to any learning and development. Some of the ideas in the personal cost view above are echoed in the models of transition, e.g. Handy's (1993), where an individual moves from denial and resistance to exploration, acceptance and commitment. There are also links here to the idea of cognitive dissonance (Festinger, 1957), which refers to the discomfort felt by learners at the discrepancy between what they already know or believe and any new information or interpretation. These can be necessary stages in anyone's journey in dealing with change – they are not necessarily negative or oppositional in the long run – but they do have the potential to be. By working in a learner-centred way you will be more likely to understand these stages and work with them positively to enable people to become more open to new or different ideas, rather than interpreting them in more negative ways and becoming a further barrier to learning.

Acknowledging that there may well be a personal cost involved for people undergoing change, that a period of transition may be required, or that dissonance is likely to happen, and accepting these as natural features of the overall process of change allow a more complete and value-based approach to enabling and leading of others through that change.

ACTIVITY **6.2**

Facilitating change

In an ideal world, what would a 'facilitative environment' to deal with the cost of learning contain or look like? In reality, what could be achieved and how?

Communities and change

Other research (e.g. a study by Vakola and Nikolaou, 2005) focuses on the impact of stress during periods of organisational change, concluding that, unless the majority of staff perceives that the organisation is developing supportive mechanisms to change, it will be a stressful experience, and stress ultimately becomes an inhibitor to change. Most importantly, this study also shows that the lack of a socially supportive environment was found to be the strongest predictor of negative attitudes to change. As change will have a different impact on each person we can see an important role for supervision here in identifying this and responding to individual learning needs, i.e. combining individual support with communal development. In effect, we can see the importance of a supportive culture of learning and for everyone to be involved in the support and enabling of others during such times. Any enabler or leader could therefore work effectively with existing groups or communities to help them enable each other too.

FURTHER READING

Healy, K. (2000) *Social Work Practices: Contemporary perspectives on change.* London: Sage.

Kotter, J.P. (1996) *Leading Change.* Boston, MA: Harvard Business School Press.

Mullins, L.J. (2005) *Management and Organisational Behaviour.* Harlow: Prentice Hall: Chapter 22.

Yukl, G. (1998) *Leadership in Organisations.* Harlow: Prentice Hall.

Chapter 7
Supervision

This chapter will help you to consider the role of formal supervision in the professional development of health and social care staff. It supports the view that learning and development are essential components of supervision and explores ways in which effective supervisory practice can maximise learning for individual supervisees and the teams in which they operate. We will make links throughout the chapter to the Supervision Framework found within the Standards for Employers and Supervision Framework Statement (SWRB, 2011) to enable you to develop your practice as a supervisor and/or manager within the new standards for social work supervision.

Brief introduction to supervision

Supervision is central to quality assurance in health and social care and is a management tool commonly used to ensure that services are first, of a good enough standard and second, responsive to service user and carer needs (Thompson, 2006; Hafford-Letchfield *et al.*, 2008). Although supervision should be about more than quality control, this function of supervision has become increasingly important in recent years. The target-driven culture in both health and social care and the findings of critical reviews of service provision have brought changes which have led to supervision in many cases becoming a conduit for performance management tools and standardised quality assurance protocols (Gould and Baldwin, 2004). However, supervision which is predominantly about quality control in its narrowest sense, dubbed 'snoopervision' by Thompson (2006), represents a rather short-sighted approach to management which fails to recognise the key importance of individual staff development and wider organisational learning to the provision of high-quality services. This issue has been recently addressed by the Social Work Reform Board (SWRB, 2010), which highlighted the central importance of critical reflection in supervision to enable social workers to develop their capacity to use their experiences to review their practice, receive feedback on performance, build emotional resilience and think reflectively about the relationships they have formed with service users and carers.

Supervision has been widely written about and most of the literature identifies four key functions. The names given to these functions vary between authors but they can be summarised as:

1. management – allocating and monitoring work, ensuring quality of practice;

2. support – providing pastoral care for the individual (not counselling);

3. education – providing support for professional development;

4. mediation – balancing the needs of the individual supervisee with the needs of the organisation; providing a channel for two-way information flow.

Most authors point to the need to keep a good balance between these four functions within supervision (Kadushin, 1976; Pritchard, 1995; Tsui, 2005; Thompson, 2006). However, the vital importance of the educative function for professionals working in today's complex and rapidly changing society has been particularly highlighted in recent literature (Gould and Baldwin, 2004; Hafford-Letchfield *et al.*, 2008). This emphasis on the educational or developmental element of supervision is reflected in the new Supervision Framework (SWRB, 2011). The framework outlines the following four key elements that must be provided in supervision for social workers:

1. support for quality decision making and interventions (through critical reflection);

2. line management and organisational accountability;

3. caseload and workload management;

4. identification of further personal learning, career and development opportunities.

The guidance that forms part of the framework makes it clear that social workers should be supported to make quality decisions and interventions by creating space in supervision for critical reflection. This should include reflection on how practice can be improved and how barriers to effective working can be minimised. By separating this element of supervision from caseload management, the SWRB is sending a clear message about the central importance it places on supervision, not only monitoring performance but also supporting the development of professional capability. The SWRB makes explicit links between the provision of good-quality supervision and the capacity of organisations to provide effective and efficient services that are responsive to the needs of service users and carers. The importance of a joined-up approach with clear links between supervision and appraisal is also stressed (see Chapter 11).

It may not always be possible or even desirable for one supervisor to meet all of a social worker's supervision needs. The SWRB (2010) has stated that social workers in child protection and adult safeguarding teams who have safeguarding and protection work as a core part of their role should normally be supervised by their line manager, who should be a registered social worker. However, social workers in multi-professional teams who do not have core protection or safeguarding roles can have the elements of supervision split between several different supervisors so long as all four elements are regularly covered within the overall supervision provision. This allows employers to adopt a more flexible approach to supervision with two or more supervisors offering support in the aspects of a worker's practice in which they have a particular expertise or leadership role. Group or peer supervision can also be considered as part of this more flexible approach (SWRB, 2010). One of the obvious considerations if responsibility for supervision is split between supervisors is how the roles and responsibilities of the supervisors will be clarified. A supervision agreement that is negotiated by and agreed with all involved will help to avoid any confusion, duplication or omissions.

In the remainder of this chapter we will focus on the educative or developmental function of supervision, covered by elements 1 and 4 of the Supervision Framework (SWRB, 2011).

Enabling learning through supervision

You can support professional learning in a number of ways through supervision.

1. *'Managerial' approaches* – performance appraisal and personal development. This is planning which results in the identification of training and development needs and facilitation of learning opportunities (within supervision or outside). This is a very important part of supervision in most health and social care organisations, often performing a central role in workforce development strategy. Partnership working between supervisors and supervisees can reduce power imbalances and encourage supervisees to take responsibility for their own learning through self-evaluation and personal target setting. Clear links are needed to induction and appraisal processes.

2. *Direct teaching* – e.g. via provision of information and advice, role modelling, shadowing, feedback on practice. This can be a very important aspect of supervision as the supervisor is traditionally a more experienced practitioner than the supervisee and should therefore be able to guide the supervisee's learning and development (Davys and Beddoe, 2009). However, in multidisciplinary teams, supervisors are not always from the same professional background as their supervisee and are therefore not necessarily professionally competent to provide this type of supervision. Some (or all) of this role may be delegated to a mentor or coach (see Chapter 8).

3. *Supporting the development of transferable skills* – supervision can provide supervisees with opportunities for debate on contentious issues and exploration of different models and theories. The ability to self-evaluate and manage own learning can also be developed with the support of the supervisor (SWRB, 2010). Skills such as creativity, critical thinking, problem solving and decision making can be encouraged to develop by the supervisor through exploration of issues and discussion regarding the supervisee's practice. The development of these skills will help supervisees gain confidence in their ability to exercise professional judgement in practice situations (Munro, 2011).

4. *Facilitating learning through critical reflection* – 'case-work' discussion has traditionally been a key part of the supervisory process in both health and social care. The supervisor's role is to support in-depth exploration and analysis of work processes from initial allocation to completion of tasks. The supervisor can achieve this by helping the supervisee to test his or her assessments, uncover assumptions and prejudices, consider alternative perspectives and approaches and identify gaps in knowledge. In healthcare professions this aspect of supervision is sometimes called clinical supervision and is often separated from management supervision and provided by an experienced colleague rather than a line manager. There are pros and cons with separating supervision in this way, which you will be able to think more about as you go on to consider the conditions that support critical reflection in supervision.

Learning through critical reflection in supervision

According to Knott and Scragg (2007: 123), supervision provides a *unique opportunity for supporting staff and providing a context for critically reflective practice*. But why is it important to provide this opportunity to learn through critical reflection within supervision?

As we have already established, it is now widely accepted that critically reflective practice is an essential component of professional service provision (DoH, 2002a; Knott and Scragg, 2007; SWRB, 2010; Munro, 2011). Supervision provides a valuable opportunity for practitioners to discuss practice and to explore alternative approaches and ideas in a safe and supported environment. Today's hectic work schedules make it more important than ever that supervision provides protected time and encouragement to reflect on practice. Without such support in supervision there is a real danger that critical reflection will become an activity forced to the margins of professional practice.

Although all practitioners are encouraged to take a critically reflective stance towards their work through their professional training (GSCC, 2005), high caseloads and other work pressures often mean that time for reflection is in short supply. Furthermore, people do not reflect on their practice just because they have been told that it is a good idea (Moon, 1999) and even when they do reflect, they usually need support to make reflection more purposeful and more critical. In exploring this issue, Argyris and Schön (1978) talk about the importance of supporting others to confront their own ideas and explore their unconscious assumptions, whilst Rutter and Brown (2012) draw attention to the dangers of solitary reflection, which can become circular and self-justifying. Ellstrom (2006, cited by Boud *et al.*, 2006) points out that there are limits to how much people can learn from experience if they are reflecting on their own. In order to analyse and evaluate a task, you need to have knowledge and understanding that enable you to identify which aspects of a task are significant and need further analysis or new learning. An effective supervisor can help a practitioner gain an in-depth understanding of a situation that enables learning and decision-making processes. Without support for reflection through supervision, practice can become routinised and there is a very real danger that practitioners will unquestioningly apply inappropriate standardised responses in complex situations (Thompson, 2000).

Conditions for supporting critical reflection in supervision

According to Moon (1999: 169), the *expression of personal material in reflection can be threatening*. When people are encouraged to reflect on their own practice there is the very real fear that they will demonstrate a lack of knowledge or expose poor practice. This fear can be made even more real in situations where supervisees feel that their practice is under particular scrutiny. Although critical reflection is now considered a basic professional skill, not all practitioners have the opportunity to engage in it. Some are not actually very good at it because they lack the skills to engage in deep reflection and look at issues from different perspectives. Facilitating critical reflection can therefore be a challenge for supervisors and one which they are often not specifically trained to deal with.

There are a number of factors which will impact on the quality of critical reflection in supervision that you need to consider.

Relationship

The quality of the relationship between the supervisee and yourself as a supervisor can have a very significant impact on depth of critical reflection and learning that takes place within supervision (Rogers, 2002). Not all supervision should or will be the same, as each supervisory relationship will be unique and will evolve over time (Beverley and Worsley, 2007). The following list outlines the issues that you need to consider:

- the impact of the power imbalance between supervisor and supervisee, which may reduce openness and honesty in discussions;

- the impact of difference between the supervisee and supervisor on the relationship and the way that this is handled by both parties. Is it openly discussed? Do the supervisee and supervisor feel accepted and valued? Do the supervisee and supervisor feel that their race, culture and gender are taken into account?

- past experience of supervision and the expectations that this brings to the new supervisory relationship for both the supervisor and supervisee;

- the extent to which expectations of supervision are shared (a supervision contract will help with this and should be an important part of building trust);

- the level of trust between supervisor and supervisee and the empathy and genuineness shown by the supervisor;

- the extent to which there is a culture for learning that provides an atmosphere of exploration and an acceptance by both parties that there are few right answers – this encourages consideration of different perspectives and options. Supervision in which the supervisor provides 'the right answer' rather than supports exploration and evaluation by the supervisee will discourage critical reflection;

- the extent to which 'safe' risk taking is encouraged to enable supervisees to discuss uncertainty and learn from errors.

Skills of the supervisor

Your skills as a supervisor will impact on the quality of supervision and the way that critical reflection is enabled (Brookfield, 1987; Gould and Baldwin, 2004; Knott and Scragg, 2007; Hafford-Letchfield *et al.,* 2008). Specific training in supervisory skills is rarely offered to new supervisors, particularly the skills required to facilitate critical reflection. There are a number of issues which you need to consider:

- relevant professional expertise, e.g. knowledge of service user group, experience of working in supervisee's job role, knowledge of legislation, relevant theory/research, knowledge of policies and procedures;

- ability to reflect critically on own practice and share reflections with supervisee. People who do not regularly reflect on their own practice are not able to support reflection in others (Moon, 1999);

- specific skills in critical analysis, critical evaluation and the use of reflective frameworks and critical questioning to enable critical reflection in others;

- use of active listening skills – these are very important skills which can be transferred from the professional arena and used within the context of supervision;

- skills in providing usable and effective feedback on the supervisee's practice. Kadushin and Harkness (2002) point out the importance of using specific statements linked to evidence when providing feedback to make it very clear which aspects of practice are good and which can be improved;

- time management in supervision sessions.

ACTIVITY **7.1**

Supervision and critical reflection

How effective do you think you are at critically reflecting on your practice?

Think of a recent example where you would have liked to have reflected more critically before you took action. What blocks existed to critical reflection in that situation? How could a competent supervisor have helped you?

Organisational context

The organisational context that you work within will impact on the extent to which you can enable critical reflection. There are several issues that you need to consider within your organisation:

- policies and procedures relating to supervision – the expectations set by the organisation and value placed on supervision;

- training for supervisors;

- openness towards questioning and new ideas – particular 'bottom-up ideas' from staff to management;

- culture for learning.

The supervisee

The supervisee will also have a significant impact on the extent of critical reflection and learning that can occur through supervision. Not all practitioners are at the same developmental stage; some find it easier than others to reflect critically on their practice and be analytical (Moon, 1999). Some are more able than others to manage their own learning and self-evaluate their practice. There are a number of factors relating to supervisees' attitudes and abilities that need to be considered:

- openness to new ideas and learning – this will depend partly on the supervisee's personal attributes but will also be affected by the context in which the supervisee is working; for example, people facing change often become resistant to new ideas (see Chapter 6);

- readiness to accept and act on feedback;

- ability to reflect critically and learn from reflections – this will vary from person to person and with an individual over time. People may have blocks to reflection on some issues even if they are generally effective reflective practitioners – this is particularly true with regard to beliefs that have been held for a long time (anchor hypotheses). People also have basic tendencies to seek out information which supports their existing views and ignore information which contradicts it, making them less critical in their reflections;

- level of self-awareness and cognitive development;

- understanding of their own professional role and relevant professional knowledge base;

- ability to take responsibility for directing own learning and self-evaluate own practice. A supervisor should support supervisees to become more self-directed as this will improve the quality of their learning (Knowles, 1990).

Strategies that can be used in supervision to enable learning through critical reflection

There are a number of ways that supervisors can support learning through critical reflection in supervision. The following list outlines some strategies that you could consider.

- *Case discussions* of current workload, focusing on issues from the case which are particularly challenging, encouraging self-evaluation of practice and action planning. Supervision can provide a safe and supportive environment for exploring alternative approaches and perspectives. It can be particularly helpful to encourage the supervisee to view the case from the service user's or carer's perspective.

- *Case studies* – using old cases or even made-up cases to enable supervisees to explore situations which are new to them in a safe and supportive environment. Soap operas can provide useful material for case studies!

- *Critical incident analysis* can provide an opportunity for supervisees to identify a critical incident and explore that incident in supervision in critical depth. The supervisor can help the supervisee to focus on what has been learnt from the incident and how practice can be developed in the future.

- *Reflective diary* – many students are now encouraged to keep reflective diaries and this can be a useful tool to encourage critical reflection in qualified workers. Excerpts from the diary can be brought to supervision to aid discussion and provide a window into the supervisee's thoughts and feelings.

- *Role plays* – although these can be very unpopular with some people, used with care they can be a useful tool in enabling supervisees to place themselves into the shoes of another person, enabling them to see a situation from the service user's perspective.

With all of the above, the use of effective critical questioning (Brookfield, 1987; Fook and Gardner, 2007) is the key to enabling the supervisee to explore cases and issues in critical depth. It will not be enough to provide the space and opportunity to reflect: you will need to support reflection actively by asking questions which challenge and unsettle without making the supervisee feel threatened and insecure. It may be helpful to consider using a model of critical reflection to provide structure by breaking the reflective process into stages. There are many different models and you may need to explore several different approaches before you find one that feels comfortable for you.

Flexible approaches to supervision

Although individual supervision has been the most common form of supervision in health and social care, there is a growing interest in peer group supervision as a supplement to, or replacement for, some elements of the more traditional approach. Peer group supervision can provide participants with rich learning opportunities in which they can explore a range of perspectives and draw, not only on a supervisor, but also on the wider expertise of their colleagues (SWRB, 2010). Including peer group supervision as part of an overall strategy can have additional benefits, such as the promotion of a team learning culture, increased team cohesion and a move towards more shared decision making. However, it is worth remembering that any form of group supervision needs skilled facilitation to ensure that all participants benefit from the process and are empowered to participate fully (see Chapter 5).

FURTHER READING

Fook, J. and Gardner, F. (2007) *Practising Critical Reflection: A resource handbook.* Maidenhead: OU Press.

Pritchard, J. (ed.) (1995) *Good Practice in Supervision.* London: Jessica Kingsley.

Tsui, M.S. (2005) *Social Work Supervision: Contexts and concepts.* London: Sage.

Chapter 8
Coaching and mentoring

Coaching and mentoring are development techniques based on one to one discussion to enhance an individual's skills, knowledge or work performance.

(Chartered Institute of Personnel and Development (CIPD), 2011)

In this chapter we consider the role of coaching and mentoring in learning and professional development. We introduce and explore the similarities and differences between the two techniques and help you consider how you can apply coaching and mentoring approaches within your workplace to improve the performance of the staff that you lead or manage. Coaching and mentoring are used in a wide variety of contexts to improve performance. Both techniques are currently receiving increased attention in health and social care as they are widely considered to be efficient and cost-effective ways of enabling both individual and organisational learning (Hafford-Letchfield *et al.*, 2008). It is common for people to feel vague about the distinction between coaching and mentoring as the terms are often used interchangeably. Although there is some considerable overlap between the two techniques, they offer distinct approaches to enabling learning, with the focus of coaching being on the achievement of short-term, specific goals, whilst mentoring has a longer-term and more generalised remit.

What is coaching?

Coaching is a time-limited one-to-one process that is set up to enable the coachee to achieve specific goals or targets. It can be provided by a line manager or by someone from outside the line management structure, such as a consultant or person from another department. Although it may be advantageous for someone who has already established an effective working relationship with the coachee to take on the role, it may be difficult for that person to provide the independent perspective that may be needed to effect change. In the private sector, coaching – particularly for managers – is commonly provided by independent people who are brought in for the purpose.

A coach is not necessarily someone who is an expert in the coachee's area of practice but will always be someone who has an expertise in coaching techniques. Coaching is a deductive process – one of drawing out knowledge and ideas from the person being coached. The primary aims of the process are to help the coachee be more analytical, think more critically and problem-solve more effectively. The process is often used to support change and can help people to move on in both their thinking and their practice. It focuses on results and how those results can be most effectively achieved.

Coaching is not about telling people how to do their job, although at times there may be some elements of teaching or advice within the role. Where this is the case the teaching and advice are generally aimed at developing coachees' own skills, knowledge and confidence by helping them to find their own solutions and not by offering ready-made answers. One of the fundamental tenets of coaching is that the coachee, not the coach, is the expert in his or her practice area and has the capacity to achieve his or her goals with the support of the coach.

How can people benefit from coaching?

There are a number of situations where short-term coaching can help workers to be more effective in their roles. Habitual ways of thinking and acting can make it very difficult for people to deal with change or cope with new situations. Coaching can provide challenge and support that enable coachees to explore, evaluate and adopt alternative approaches that increase their capability, help them to deal with uncertainty and adapt to change. As such, providing access to coaching as part of a learning and development strategy can enable employers to meet some of the standards for supervision proposed by the Social Work Reform Board (SWRB, 2010) and address the issues raised in the Munro report (Munro, 2011) with respect to supporting the development of professional confidence and judgement.

As a manager you may consider providing workers with access to coaching support at times when they are facing significant change such as on promotion, following reorganisation or at any point that you identify the need to adopt a new or updated approach to practice. Coaching can be particularly helpful as a short-term strategy to support workers who are not meeting the expectations of an organisation or in situations where a member of staff is in conflict with others or with the organisation as a whole. A good example of when coaching can be effective is following a serious case review when a coach can support workers to understand and act on the findings – hopefully, resulting in changes to practice. However, although coaching is now widely used within many organisations and is seen as a cost-effective solution to a range of problems, it is only one of many possible approaches that can be used to support learning and development. As such, it may need to be used in combination with other longer-term strategies, such as supervision, involvement in communities of practice and other forms of continuing professional development. One of the key factors that should be considered with the provision of any specific support for learning is the personal choice and preferred learning style of the learner (CIPD, 2011).

Coaching can be of benefit to both individuals and organisations because it provides a framework within which they can:

- negotiate, agree and monitor the achievement of objectives;
- identify, plan and facilitate new learning;
- challenge assumptions, prejudices and habitual thinking;
- support problem solving and decision making;
- support metacognitive development (skills such as learning how to learn, improving critical thinking);
- enable people to recognise and empathise with other perspectives;

- enable the transfer of learning/skills/knowledge from one situation to another;
- encourage people to take responsibility for their learning and their practice.

Setting up a coaching relationship

Core principles

If a coaching relationship is to achieve its objectives it must adhere to the following core principles:

- a commitment to the support of the individual (focus on the individual, not on the organisation);
- a relationship built on truth, openness and trust and equality;
- a shared understanding that the coachee retains responsibility for the outcomes;
- a shared belief that the coachee is capable of better results than s/he is currently achieving;
- a focus on what the coachee thinks and experiences.

(Starr, 2003, cited by Mullins, 2005: 419)

When coaching is provided by a line manager within supervision there are some obvious challenges with the application of the core principles described above. Most supervision is provided within a hierarchical system, although this is not always true of clinical supervision in health settings (Rolfe *et al.*, 2001). Where a hierarchy is apparent it will inevitably mean that one of the fundamental principles will not be met as there can never be equality within the relationship. However, Thompson (2006) does not necessarily see this as a barrier to successful coaching within supervision, pointing out that it is often the line manager who is in the best position to support and enable learning. He believes that, even if the supervisory relationship is hierarchical, the coaching elements within supervision can be set up to be more equal through, for example, the establishment of a culture in which the coach and coachee learn from each other and in which the coachee is recognised as the 'expert' in his or her own practice. If you do decide to offer coaching support to a member of your team you will need to think carefully about how you can ensure that you do not compromise the value of the relationship through the inappropriate use of power whilst enabling learning.

Coaching agreement

In order to ensure that coaching sessions are focused on the needs of the coachee and that clear objectives are set and achieved, it is helpful if coaching relationships are governed by a written agreement which as a minimum should include the following:

- where and when sessions should take place;
- how long sessions should last;
- how long the coaching arrangement will last;
- arrangements for cancelling meetings;
- agreement on how progress will be reviewed;

- coachee's objectives;

- boundaries of the relationship, e.g. whether there will be contact between sessions;

- what happens if the relationship is not working;

- what happens if the coach is sick or on long periods of leave.

If coaching is part of supervision, a supervision agreement may already be in place which covers most of these areas. It will, however, still be useful to agree objectives, timescales and methods of review that will be specific to the coaching objectives within the supervisory process. Whether part of overall supervision or not, a brief record should be kept of coaching sessions which sets out main areas of discussion and any action points agreed.

Providing a structure in coaching sessions

Although all coaches will develop their own personal style of working and each coaching relationship will have individual characteristics, Mullins (2005) suggests that it may be useful to use a framework within coaching sessions to provide structure and focus. The following framework is drawn from Whitemore:

> *The GROW model*
>
> *Goals – what does the coachee want to achieve? How do they want to feel at the end of sessions and at the end of the period of coaching?*
>
> *Reality – what is the context, what are the problems, how have the problems been handled in the past?*
>
> *Options – what are the possible actions? Which are most attractive and most achievable? What has worked in the past?*
>
> *Wrap up – what actions are needed? What will success look like? What about plan B?*
>
> (Whitemore, 1996, cited by Mullins, 2005: 419)

It is unlikely that this model or any other model will work for you without some adaptation. To help you think more about how you can use a coaching model within a coaching relationship, reflect on your own experiences and do some reading about other models currently in use (see, for example, Egan's Skilled Helper Model in Connor and Pokora, 2012). What elements of the various models you have read about or experienced do you like and what don't you like? Can you combine several models to make one that fits more comfortably with your own personal style and approach?

Skills required by an effective coach

In the introduction to this section it was stated that to be an effective coach you don't need to be an expert in the coachee's field of work. This is a point of view that some people would question and, as with most contentious issues, there are pros and cons to having a personal expertise in the coachee's area of practice which you may wish to consider for yourself.

Although there is a debate about the need for specific practice-based expertise, most people would agree that effective coaches need to have developed skills and attributes to equip them for their role. Many of these skills and attributes are the same as those required for enabling any form of learning, but there is a particularly strong overlap with the skills required to facilitate critically reflective learning. They include:

- good communication skills;
- active listening skills;
- critical and open questioning skills;
- an ability to create a supportive and confidence-inspiring environment;
- skills in critical reflection and a commitment to reflexivity;
- self-awareness;
- a commitment to own learning and development and an openness to learning and new ideas;
- an interest in enabling the learning of others;
- an ability to suspend judgement and listen with an open mind;
- an ability to enable others to identify strengths and weaknesses and negotiate clear and achievable objectives for development;
- empathy;
- good feedback skills;
- empowerment and enablement skills;
- assertiveness and honesty.

Thompson (2006) describes the requirements of a coach in terms of skills, knowledge and values, stating that coaches require as a minimum:

- *knowledge*: of how adults learn and the blocks that can exist to learning;
- *skills*: in communicating and engaging with others;
- *values*: commitment to learning and working to empower and respect diversity.

Is coaching always provided one to one and face to face?

Although the most common model of coaching is one to one and face to face, other coaching models exist, such as group coaching (where groups of individuals have common goals) and telephone or email coaching.

What is mentoring?

Mentoring is generally considered to have a wider remit than coaching but may incorporate elements of coaching within broader developmental objectives, e.g. when a mentor supports a mentee with the achievement of a particular objective as part of the work undertaken with the mentee. One of the most significant differences between coaching and mentoring is that a mentor should *always* be someone who is skilled and experienced in the mentee's field of work and should therefore be able to provide direct support with the development of the mentee's knowledge, skills and confidence (Neary, 2000; Mullins, 2005; Connor and Pokora, 2012). Familiarity with the mentee's work environment is also very important. Mentors are often provided for newly qualified workers or workers taking on new areas of responsibility to help them develop the specific skills and knowledge they require to undertake the new role.

Mentoring is a means of ensuring that knowledge and skills are passed from experienced members of staff to those who are less experienced and can be an effective way of supporting a culture of learning within the workplace. Mentoring can also support networking and interprofessional working as mentors can help mentees identify important contacts and facilitate introductions to key people. Although mentors are always more experienced members of staff than mentees, the mentor relationship should not be hierarchical (Connor and Pokora, 2007), and it is therefore more usual for a mentor to be a more experienced colleague than a manager. It is sometimes described as a learning alliance to demonstrate that the relationship is about working in partnership to support learning, principally of the mentee but also of the mentor (Thompson, 2006).

Mentor arrangements are normally longer-term than coaching relationships and will often involve more frequent contact, including access to the mentor's support in between any formal mentor sessions that take place. The objectives for the relationship are likely to evolve over time as the mentee develops skills and confidence and shifts focus from one area of practice to another.

Benefits of mentoring

For the employer

- improved communication within the organisation;
- increased motivation as staff feel more valued and supported;
- cost-effective, on-the-job support for learning and development.

For mentors

- new skills in enabling adult learning;
- improved job satisfaction and self-esteem, as skills are recognised and valued;
- new perspectives and new learning through working with the mentee;
- improved communication with others in the organisation.

For mentees

- improved self-confidence and motivation;
- fuller understanding of the organisation's objectives, policies and procedures;

- development of skills and knowledge relevant to the job;

- workplace support and advice when needed both informally and formally;

- personal and career development.

Setting up a mentoring relationship

Most of the material covered in the section on setting up a coaching relationship, above, applies equally to mentoring. It is just as important that the terms of reference, boundaries and objectives of the relationship are set out in a written agreement, that mentor sessions have a clear structure and the skills and attributes of a mentor will be those of a coach with the additional proviso that the mentor must be occupationally competent in the mentee's area of work.

However, mentoring is different from coaching. It has a wider remit and will use a wider range of methods to support and enable learning to take place. This will often include:

- direct teaching through the provision of information;

- clarification and explanation of policies, procedures and legislation;

- working through case studies to develop understanding;

- sharing material such as reports and records to help the mentee understand the organisation's requirements;

- shadowing by the mentee of the mentor's work;

- joint working to aid the development of skills and confidence;

- reflective discussions in mentor sessions;

- objective setting;

- recommendations for reading and research;

- setting of learning and development tasks.

The support needs of coaches and mentors

People who take on the responsibilities of coaching and mentoring others will need to be supported with the performance of their roles, particularly whilst they are inexperienced or when taking on any new responsibilities. Although many of the skills used in these roles are a core part of the everyday skills base of health and social care professionals, support may be needed to enable workers to transfer these skills into their coaching or mentoring roles. Specific training should also be provided to help with the development of new knowledge and skills that are specific to the role, such as the facilitation of reflective learning and knowledge about how adults learn. Specific ongoing supervision and support will also be required.

ACTIVITY 8.1

Considering coaching and mentoring skills

Consider the above skills and attributes with respect to your own practice. If you were to take on the role of a coach or mentor, what would be your areas of strength? Which aspects of your practice would need further development?

Coaches and mentors as leaders

An important aspect of the role of coaches and mentors is leadership. Leadership in this context is not about simply encouraging people to follow but rather is about empowering individuals to develop their personal and professional capability. Mentoring and coaching, when done well, will foster creativity and innovation and will help build the skills needed by professionals to deal with complexity and uncertainty (Hafford-Letchfield *et al.*, 2008).

Coaching and mentoring provide highly individualised ways of supporting learning in the workplace. Because learners retain responsibility for their own learning, with the support of the coach or mentor, they are encouraged to develop a sense of professional responsibility for their lifelong learning. Coaching and mentoring can therefore be seen as effective ways of supporting the development of professional capabilities at all stages of learning and career development.

FURTHER READING

Brockbank, A. and McGill, I. (2002) *Facilitating Reflective Learning Through Mentoring and Coaching.* London: Kogan Page.

Foster-Turner, J. (2005) *Coaching and Mentoring in Health and Social Care: The essential manual for professionals and organisations.* Oxford: Radcliff.

Hafford-Letchfield, T., Leonard, K., Begum, N. and Chick, N. (2008) *Leadership and Management in Social Care.* London: Sage.

Chapter 8 includes useful case studies which provide examples of how coaching can be used.

Chapter 9
Group learning

This chapter looks at being involved in the training and development of others in a group with the main emphasis on delivering group learning events. Types of training are listed, and the overall process is covered before detailing various key areas and factors for consideration as an enabler and leader.

Types of training and development

As stated earlier, there is a wide range of group learning and training events, some more formal than others. It is important to recognise that formal ones, although possibly more familiar and standard, should not be chosen for that reason alone. The idea is to understand the issues so that the most appropriate ways to meet training needs are chosen and used.

Formal planned learning:

- in-house training sessions; presentations; workshops;
- university-based education.

Informal or semiformal learning:

- projects;
- day-to-day experiences;
- on-the-job learning;
- supervision (see Chapter 7);
- team meetings;
- informal discussions.

Issues to consider:

- effectiveness – learning objectives may be non-existent, poorly defined, overambitious, diffuse;
- usefulness – how is the content and delivery expected to result in achieving specific outcomes, e.g. practice or reflection time?
- applicability – some consideration of possible connections to work practice is necessary to ensure both short- and long-term effects on behaviour and performance;

- evaluation – a comprehensive approach to measuring and judging outcomes and enabling the transfer of learning into workplace practice can overcome many of the above limitations.

Formal education and training contribute to only a small proportion of learning at work. In particular, developing understanding of situations, colleagues, the team and the organisation are examples where learning occurs while working. Some of these more informal areas could benefit from being made formal, e.g. for induction purposes (see Chapter 10). As discussed in our first section, professionals, in particular, develop their own ways of understanding and dealing with the complexity of their work, informally building up a store of experiences and scenarios which allows them to develop their decision-making skills. This expertise building still needs to be kept under review via interaction and questioning from others, otherwise uncritical practice may begin to be followed (Fook *et al.,* 2000).

There is a need to ensure that staff are able to capture, measure and accredit such informal learning when it contributes to the development of their role or updating of practice and knowledge for continuing professional development (CPD) evaluation. Staff can keep portfolios for recording, analysing and planning learning, and to provide a continuous record of formal and informal learning. They can include:

- reflections on practice;

- notes from supervision or appraisal;

- learning achievements;

- project involvement;

- feedback from users, carers, colleagues, external partners;

- putting more formal learning into practice.

As mentioned earlier, neither the content nor the amount of CPD undertaken is specified within the Health and Care Professions Council's social work registration requirements, but as there will be an emphasis on the impact CPD activities have on practice, it is important to have an awareness of how such learning impacts and makes a difference to practice and to service quality.

Organisational and contextual factors can impede or promote informal learning, but the problem is this is done in very insidious ways which are difficult to identify, let alone either maximise or address. The factors which appear to be more conducive to informal learning are flatter hierarchies, more widely distributed managerial responsibilities and high involvement of employees in service and process development. As a leader or enabler of such learning it would be important to have an awareness of these and other factors (such as access to learning resources and links to organisational networks, e.g. supervision, team meetings) within your own context.

The overall process

There are many different levels and types of training, but a generalised process can be seen which covers the planning, delivery and evaluation of training or group learning events. Each stage has an important role to play and training can fail if one or more of these stages is missed out or ignored. We will not cover each of these as a sequence but we will be looking at key areas and aspects of this process.

1. Assess and agree training needs – consider how to involve people in identifying and agreeing relevant, aligned training; consider organisational and professional values.

2. Create training/development aims and objectives – consider the level of content, and try to break down the training or learning requirement into manageable elements. What exactly do you want people to be able to do after the event?

3. Consider the people attending and their experience and needs, the possible range of their learning styles plus any relevant learning theories or principles you wish to adhere to, e.g. adult learning principles.

4. Using information gained from the stages above, decide on the method and approach; plan the event; design materials and activities; plan any necessary support or extra resourcing before and after the event. Off-the-peg training packages may be reviewed and chosen as well.

5. Either deliver the training or liaise with the people who are delivering it, and ensure methods or resources are in place so learning can be enabled.

6. Evaluate the effectiveness and worth of the training. Use the aims and objectives as measurable outcomes, e.g. meeting immediate needs, relevancy, but also consider less measurable outcomes, e.g. ongoing usefulness to the team, style of teaching.

7. Plan necessary changes for the future – evaluate all the above stages for what might have been achieved more effectively.

Key area: understanding and meeting training/learning needs

The first stage can be one of the most important in making sure training and development events are relevant and meaningful for people. Information gathering and analysis can take place from a variety of sources and meet maintenance as well as the development needs of individuals and the organisation.

Potential sources include:

- induction;
- job description;
- appraisal;
- supervision;
- team discussions/meetings;
- policy/legislative directives;
- informal conversations which highlight a general need;
- previous training events – further dissemination.

When discussing previous events with individuals it may be possible to identify learning that can be disseminated further, or shared with the team. This may include asking the team member to run a team training event, a valuable exercise which can carry individual learning into team practice. One way of ensuring the relevance and applicability of training to practice is involving experienced practitioners and specialists in training design and delivery. This involvement can have a big impact on the quality of training that is offered, so exploring whether you and your team are contributing fully to training, and determining what might be done to encourage this, is very worthwhile. This is especially the case as involvement in training can be very rewarding for individuals and can open up career options that allow practitioners to have a beneficial impact on training and education. Encouraging team members to develop areas of expertise as a team resource to share with others is also a good way of building a community of practice.

ACTIVITY **9.1**

Involvement in training

How much of a proactive role do staff have in this regard? How does this affect their learning plans and the organisation's learning culture?

Key area: designing and delivering training and development

There are two aspects to designing and delivering group learning; see Chapter 2 for more detail about the theories mentioned here.

Making explicit the underpinning principles and values being adhered to

Some underpinning key principles for any type of learning can be taken from Knowles's (1980) adult learning principles. These provide a way of valuing learners as mature, self-directing adults who bring their own experience and knowledge. Others may be gleaned from your own experience, e.g. interpersonal communication; anti-discriminatory and ethical practice.

Identify and plan the methods and techniques

Particular methods and techniques can be gleaned from learning theories, e.g. experiential learning cycles show the need to include activities for reflecting, generalising and planning as well as the 'doing'; reflective learning models show the need to include questioning and challenging activities.

More general methods can also be applied; for example, James Atherton (2011b) notes the use of broad principles such as advance organisers, scaffolding, models and metaphors for more instructional teaching.

Advance organisers

These are simply devices used in the introduction of a topic which enable learners to orient themselves to it so that they can locate where any particular bit of input fits in and how it links with what they already know. They may be handouts outlining a session, statements of objectives, diagrams or clear introductory remarks. They give the students confidence that you know where you are going, as well as helping them to get a handle on the session and to see when and how new material is being introduced.

Practice ideas

- When designing a learning event, try and plan the structure before you work on the detail.

- When doing a PowerPoint presentation, use the first slide or a handout to show how the complete presentation fits together.

Scaffolding
The teacher provides the structure within which learners can build their learning. This includes engaging learners' interest, demonstrating ideas, progressing from the simple to the complex, organising material, summarising, providing feedback, and so on.

Practice ideas

- Show any topic areas you are covering within the bigger picture, e.g. as a diagram, or add spaces where learners can write in their own areas of knowledge or interest.

- Think about all the stages when presenting material or content – what else do learners need to help them understand? Before telling learners something allow them time to work out the significance for themselves or after telling them something allow time to work practically with the idea, and always provide feedback on how people are doing.

Models, metaphors and analogies: structuring new ideas
With simple ideas you can start with the easy models or concepts to explain before elaborating and moving on to examples that are closer to the real world. With more complex ideas it is better to start with the concrete, real-life example before you talk about the ideas conceptually. Using analogy ('something is like something else because . . .') can be effective but also needs care because analogies can be so powerful that learners get hooked on them and may not see where the analogy doesn't fit. Using metaphors needs even more care as you are saying that one thing is something else.

Practice ideas

- Using the analogy of being on 'automatic pilot' to illustrate habitual practice.

Key area: enabling the learning within training and development activities

Working critically with adult learning principles

We can, and should, endeavour to work to adult learning principles (Knowles, 1980), but as we saw earlier, they do not always take account of real-world situations or problems (Table 9.1).

When leading or designing your own group learning events it is useful to look at what you would like your approaches to be, but immediately to identify the issues and potential barriers to achieving them. 'Real-world' issues cannot be changed but at least acknowledging them will

Table 9.1 Adult learning principles and critical views

Principles	More critical views
Relevancy – adults need to know why they must learn something	In our own minds there isn't always a 'good enough' reason why we are told we have to learn something new
Self-direction – adults are responsible for their own learning	Many adults would prefer someone else to tell them what to do, especially when they have heavy workloads or are anxious novices trying to get it 'right'
Adults have greater, and more varied, experience which serves as a rich resource of learning	Experience can also be a barrier if it's the wrong kind or has promoted only concrete, routine thinking
Adult motivation is largely internal, such as self-esteem, quality of life and job satisfaction	As we know, motivation levels are extremely variable in health and social care!

show learners that you are in the 'real world', and if you are aware of these issues you can try to take account of them creatively in your planning and design of the event.

Learner-centredness

We can revisit some of the values we discussed earlier for leading and enabling others at this point. A leader or enabler needs to allow for the individual and group variations in learning, and acknowledge the function and importance of the learning environment. By working to the facilitative and supportive values embedded within adult learning principles and being aware of the issues as well, learners become people with needs and anxieties but also participative thinkers who can contribute and add extra value to the learning experience. The idea that providing content and material for learners is sufficient for learning to occur is not really justified. As a leader or enabler of learning you do need to work from a different perspective and create the learning experience or opportunity, working from the learner's perspective. There are general principles to follow to enable learners to make the learning their own.

- Ensure exploration and discussion from the learner's viewpoint.

- Allow choice.

- Build on personal knowledge and experience.

- Ensure application to the learner's situations.

- Draw out general principles from specific learning so they are usable in other contexts.

- Give corrective feedback.

- Allow time for reflective opportunities.

Levels of learning

If we revisit the different stages and levels of learning we can see that they involve different thinking processes: from simple, more mechanistic levels of remembering to being able to break knowledge apart, put it together, judge or measure it, and even create it:

- recognition and recall – memorise, identify, recognise (remembering);
- comprehension – understanding;
- analysis – breaking knowledge down into parts;
- synthesis – putting together with other knowledge to form new concepts; and applying;
- evaluation – assess the value of the new knowledge in respect of needs and aim;
- creating.

It is suggested that one cannot effectively address the 'higher' levels until the 'lower' ones have been achieved, so someone will not be expected to be able to evaluate something critically unless that person has first understood it. This has significant implications for setting objectives at the right level and also for the sequence and structuring of the learning event and its materials.

Levels of learning are also associated with deep and surface approaches to learning. Approaches are not personal attributes and people are able to adopt any approach. The one they adopt (probably unconsciously) will be related to their perception of the task and their previous experience. A surface approach focuses on acquisition and memorising of information, facts and concepts in isolation and a deep approach focuses on meaning, understanding and application of knowledge.

By knowing the level and the approach you wish learners to adopt you can design activities or materials in ways which will foster this perception of the task. In other words, if you only describe one idea on a topic you cannot then expect learners to compare it critically to others. They will more than likely believe either that this is the only idea that can be worthwhile or that this is the one you want them to remember and use or reproduce.

Ways to raise the level of learning

Is a presentation offering bullet-pointed facts the best way to engage someone's interest, motivation or curiosity? Activities and discussions which get people engaging with the ideas and material are much better ways to do this. The use of questions is also crucial here – they need to stimulate and develop creative and critical thoughts by motivating curiosity and interest. Think about the types of question that are likely to stimulate people's curiosity and how they differ from those that are likely to stifle it. Use the adult learning principles to look further at why this might happen.

Learning in groups

Advantages

- People learn really well from and with other people – not just because they bring different ideas or experiences but also because they bring questions and challenges.

- Groups can satisfy the need for security and belonging.

- The group whole becomes more than the sum of the parts.

Disadvantages

- Dominant and quiet members:
  o alter the dynamics of the group;
  o affect the output.

- Distractions occur more easily.

- Large numbers can stop individuals participating.

Issues for consideration

- Composition and size – do you need to decide in advance who is going to work with whom?

- Level of autonomy given – are you giving them things to do by themselves or with your help?

- Ensure the learning environment works best so that interaction between people can flourish and they can use their normal social and interpersonal skills, e.g. think about the layout of the room.

- Output of the group – how is it best to value/share the work each group has done?

- Support and resources – what do they need to do the work?

- Do not abandon them but interact as appropriate to the task, and be available for advice or clarification.

- How is it best to monitor what is taking place?

- Capitalising on the outcomes – this is where many fail! Any insights gained through a group activity need to be taken further through additional discussion or activities – not just to reiterate key points but also to allow important connections and links to be made, especially to future practice. Think deep rather than surface learning here (Marton and Saljo, 1976).

Key area: sharing and dissemination of learning

As discussed earlier, the idea of sharing and disseminating is at the heart of any community or practice or culture of learning and so it is important to maximise opportunities for this.

Attendees and teams

When staff attend group learning events their experience becomes a resource that could be used for the benefit of the rest of the team. As seen above, in discussing the learning benefits of previous events with an individual it may be possible to identify the learning that can be disseminated further. Use of team meetings and other events, or even supervision, may be appropriate vehicles for this. The social context created by a co-operative approach to learning and development can enhance the motivation and commitment of learners. In this way teams can help individuals transfer their skills, knowledge and understanding between contexts and also expose individuals to different strategies for making those connections. Individuals learn what types of learning will be useful to share with colleagues and they also learn about where and from whom further knowledge could be gained.

Peer learning groups (Winter and Maisch, 1996)

These create open, safe but committed spaces for learning and its dissemination, allowing exploration of possibilities, building trust and therefore self-confidence (reiterating ideas seen in Chapter 5). Tutors here act as facilitators for staff sharing their learning, offering mutual support and challenge. There can be a similarity in members' practice or work but also differences in their individual resources (e.g. knowledge, experience) that create a dynamic environment. By sharing and listening to the ideas of others, members can reframe the potential significance for themselves. The group needs to create its own sense of trust with interpersonal and teamwork skills, but the facilitator (or enabler/leader) also needs to manage and dispel any anxieties or emotional tension, from both the workplace and those inherent in the learning and development process itself. Anxiety and fear have a huge negative impact on the ability to learn and it can be seen that mutually supportive interaction is what is required for effective learning to take place. The workplace does not easily foster the type of relationship which provides this form and level of support, and so a different type of relationship may need to be established to provide this 'space for learning'.

Key area: evaluation

At the end of any training, whether you are a participant, an enabler or a leader, you will probably just want to get on with the next thing. However, without evaluation there is no chance of any improvement. Evaluation starts with feedback and so the type of questions asked are crucial. Knowing the range and level of questions available is useful to avoid them being bland, irrelevant and useless, and get to what you would really like to know, either managerially or as an enabler of learning.

A useful and practical framework for evaluating training in social care developed by Skills for Care, and discussed further in Gray *et al.* (2010b), uses a series of levels for evaluating training.

Level 1: reactions to the learning process;

Level 2: learning outcomes;

Level 3: individual outcomes or application of learning;

Level 4: organisational outcomes;

Level 5: stakeholder's outcomes.

Other factors to consider

Time

Those undertaking training or education in the workplace need the time to do it, but many managers and leaders find it difficult to sustain a sense of the importance of the training and development of their staff. Time allocation and caseload reduction should be agreed upon and organised well in advance of any formal learning events – but as we know this can start to go wrong very easily, so perhaps back-up plans B and C might also be arranged!

Meaningfulness

Unless the learning process addresses the real issues and contradictions that practitioners face, then it will be of limited value. Also, a careful balance needs to be reached in terms of concentrating on the emotional dimensions of practice and the focus on methods, skills and tasks (Lefevre, 2005, cited by Hafford-Letchfield *et al.,* 2008: 111). Finally, it's a good idea for managers and leaders of those doing the training to try and keep their own personal and professional knowledge up to date too.

FURTHER READING

There are many other ideas readily available on web pages to show educators how to present information using various methods, e.g. PowerPoint, avoiding 'death by bullet point', handouts, use of whiteboards.

Lishman, J. (2011) *Social Work Education and Training*. London: Jessica Kingsley.

Rogers, A. (2002) *Teaching Adults*. Maidenhead: McGraw Hill/Open University.

Chapter 10
Induction and probation

This chapter considers how the induction of new people in the workplace can be facilitated either by a line manager or by someone with delegated responsibility for providing leadership and enabling learning during an induction period.

Induction and probation: a crucial opportunity to influence and empower

Induction and the probationary period are best seen as the start of the relationship between your organisation and your new member of staff, mediated by you and your team. Like the initial stages of any relationship, it will strongly influence the later stages, so it deserves an attention that it sometimes does not receive. The recent newly qualified social worker (NQSW) provision and the proposals for an assessed and supported year in employment (ASYE) that will replace it recognise this importance.

This early period could also be described as formative in that it shapes the behaviours, perspectives and understanding of the new staff member and sets the learning agenda. It will, therefore, impact on that individual's motivation, effectiveness and well-being in the longer term. However, this is not to say that it is about ensuring that the new staff member 'fits in'. This is to assume that the new person must accommodate you. This may be how you wish to proceed, but what will this be saying about your leadership style and team culture to the new staff member?

Instead, it is better seen as a period of initial negotiation, where the new team member gets to know you and your team, understands requirements and how you like to work, but you also get to know the new person and what it is that is going to make it a rewarding working experience for him or her, giving that individual a chance to shape his or her working experience and find a place in the team. Seen in this way it is of mutual benefit. It can also avoid the organisation wasting resources investing in new members of staff who are better suited to another field or setting, and avoids them wasting time in an organisation to which they cannot be committed or comfortable.

Induction is also a point of transition. NQSWs are taking a first crucial step into qualified practice; others may be leaving a team where they were comfortable and effective to take on a new situation, role and relationships, of which they may know very little. So they will be anxious, they will want to impress and establish relationships but they will probably be feeling disoriented and deskilled. They may even be grieving for the friends and the role they have left behind. So induction and probation offer the opportunity to make links to carry the transition, to help new staff members reflect on their achievements and identify skills they can transfer and the relationships and practices that work for them.

In some cases you will be inducting staff who have little experience in social work and are not qualified. In this instance the responsibility is greater because you will be introducing them to the essential values, knowledge and skills that underpin social care. You will be welcoming them into the profession and equipping them with the expertise they need to do the job – so the induction will need to be more intense, providing further support and learning opportunities.

Probation is equally formative. It offers the first opportunity for staff members to be appraised. It is the time to familiarise them with your appraisal system. It offers the opportunity to rehearse how their performance will be assessed and determine their rights and responsibilities. Crucially it is their first opportunity to work with you and determine whether you are fair and methodical in making judgements that will affect the rest of their career, and how you approach the process, e.g. whether you create opportunities for dialogue or dominate it.

You may be in an organisation that has a planned induction and probationary period. This could be seen as a bonus, in that it offers a good reminder of the essentials and often provides you with some help from others and gives the activity some attention and resources. However, given what we have just stated, it can too easily become a standardised routine that offers little opportunity for either the staff member or your team to express themselves. The worst scenario involves a mixture of centrally managed corporate training events that have no relationship to their actual role, and someone working through an induction checklist as if it is something to be got out of the way as quickly as possible. Crucially, it can mean that you and your team are not able to have any influence over what may be a colleague's most important work experience, in that it sets the foundation for everything else. If you think back to your own experiences of induction you can consider the factors that were helpful and those that hindered your transition into a new role.

We will make some points about managing the standardised induction later, but for now we can try and identify the key outcomes for induction and the probationary period. Given our points above we will emphasise the 'softer' relationship aspects by putting them first and present the process so that it is person-centred. That is not to say that we do not think that the more task-focused outcomes are not crucial. It is just not much point having someone who is fully briefed on procedures but who feels alienated and excluded.

Induction and probation: the essential outcomes

Induction and probation should enable new members of staff to:

- set the foundation for an effective working relationship with you;
- begin to establish for themselves a place in the team;

- manage the transition into their new working environment, transferring skills and knowledge into their new environment;

- make contact with key co-providers, partners and community resources and begin to build relationships with them;

- experience the core workplace activities, e.g. case planning, reviews, conferences, supervision, team meetings, allocation of caseload;

- understand health and safety requirements and their responsibilities and know how to keep themselves safe;

- complete personnel/human resources (HR) requirements, e.g. understand and have signed the contract, reviewed job description and responsibilities and conditions of service, provided documentation, e.g. qualifications, completed police checks and have car insurance checked;

- be aware of staff welfare services and have sorted out union membership, pension arrangements and child care arrangements;

- meet any special needs they might have, e.g. physical disability, learning needs, second language, unfamiliar culture;

- fit in with office or establishment everyday working procedures and processes and be introduced to key facilities, e.g. working hours, signing in and out, staff facilities, travel claims, leave arrangements;

- appreciate the values of the team and the organisation and its objectives, including current business or service plans;

- understand key organisational policies and procedures;

- understand the structure of the organisation and make contact with key people within the organisation;

- review their previous training and development and work experiences and establish their learning needs during induction and beyond;

- if they are new to social work/care, acquire the values, knowledge and skills they need to do their job;

- demonstrate their competence in the job.

If, at this point, you are not feeling slightly daunted, then you have not grasped the enormity of the task. However, although induction can be an unsatisfactory experience, it is often reported as being helpful and well managed; people clearly establish themselves and do well in our organisations, so we are often already succeeding. This is simply an opportunity to review and improve induction. So how do we manage such a complex and demanding task?

Mobilising resources to meet the needs of new members of staff

As with most things you manage, you are not alone and do not need to do it all yourself. You have some key responsibilities, not the least of which is co-ordinating the overall experience; however, you have some resources you can mobilise to help achieve the required outcomes. They are:

- the person being inducted;
- the immediate team;
- the wider team;
- organisational provision;
- learning resources you can draw on or develop;
- Common Induction Standards (for care workers).

Whilst the principles will apply to your management of all the different aspects of training and development, we can look at each of these in turn and explore how you might use them when managing induction.

Enabling the person being inducted

A very good place to start is to allow the person being inducted to take control of his or her own induction process. Accepting the earlier points we considered, about not being too organisationally focused, the same is also true in reverse. New staff members have a professional responsibility for their induction and should seek to accommodate the needs of the team and the organisation; as we have suggested it is an opportunity for negotiation and for dialogue, but on both sides.

Unfortunately there is a problem. New staff members may have no idea at all what is expected of them, what induction is for and what the likely problems might be. Their previous experiences, including qualifying training, may well not have prepared them. However, this can be dealt with by discussing the induction process with new staff members, judging what they understand and have learnt from previous experience, and allowing them to contribute as much as possible. It may well help to share with them some of our thinking so far on the importance, the outcomes and the problems of induction. Bear in mind that one day they may be in your place managing or contributing to the process for others.

Even given the most limited of experiences, it will be possible to ensure that new staff members take considerable responsibility. With the outcomes or objectives of induction and probation explained, they can take responsibility for ensuring key actions happen and reviewing and evaluating their experiences. Sometimes they can take responsibility for key objectives. For instance, they can talk to members of the team, determine the key contacts they use and arrange to meet them. Whilst new staff members cannot do it all, it is reasonable to argue that the more control they have the better; it is easy to underestimate what they can do for themselves and the value of them doing it. For instance, in talking to team members about key contacts and resources, and introducing themselves, they can get a lot more than they would from a pre-set visiting schedule arranged by someone else. It just needs someone like yourself to ensure they are coping and that it is happening as planned.

Also, remember that they have previous experiences that can be drawn on in helping them shape their induction. Ask them what their learning needs/development plan was when they were last appraised or assessed. Ask what they want from supervision and how they like to be supervised. Check out their experience of appraisal and continuing professional development, what works for them or doesn't work. Try and identify the areas of expertise they will bring to the team.

It is also worth remembering that induction can be quite exhausting because so much is new. There is a limit to what new staff members can absorb, so try not to make induction too action-packed and give them some quiet time for reflection. Providing debriefs with you at various points also encourages reflection and allows you to respond to concerns or questions as well as help them interpret what they have seen. Sharing these initial experiences can also help build trust and their working relationship with you, which, as we saw earlier, is the essential underpinning to a meaningful person-centred approach to enabling learning.

ACTIVITY *10.1*

Supporting induction

Consider ways that you could support new staff members being inducted to get the most out of the induction experiences that they organise with your guidance. How will they know what questions they should be asking and what information they will need to find out? How will they evaluate and make sense of the information that they receive?

Involving your immediate team

Your team is a rich resource, so involving them in induction is crucial. This also helps the new team member feel welcome and build relationships. This becomes essential if you want to develop the team as a community of practice (see Chapter 5). If you are to engage your team in the induction process it is essential that they can see how important it is. This means that you may need to 'sell' it to them to make it meaningful. You may find they have already identified its importance and are therefore enthusiastic to contribute and support colleagues; nevertheless, some team discussion and a review of some of the points we have discussed could help.

Once they are engaged there is a lot you can delegate. For instance, individual team members can take responsibility for planning with, and supporting, a new colleague in an aspect of induction drawn from the objectives above, e.g. allowing the new team member to shadow them for some key workplace activities such as case planning. You will need to make judgement calls about their experience and suitability for certain tasks, but if induction is a team event, with its purpose understood and its responsibilities shared, it is more likely to be successful. Also identifying together, for instance, the network of partners and provision the team use (to produce a map of the service network) can be useful information sharing and offer some valuable insights.

This is not to take the responsibility away from you. You must ensure that induction is successful and determine its nature. However, if you are an enabling and participative team leader, a reasonable position would be that if you have been successful in developing the team, then an effective induction will happen even if you are not there to manage it!

Unfortunately the converse is also true. If you have a relatively new team you will have to be more directive and offer more yourself. Also, if you have some 'difficult' characters in the team you will need to protect your staff member a little from them. As we discussed earlier, most work-based learning is informal and/or experiential and so this also needs to be managed. Sometimes new team members can be seen as an opportunity to make a point or to influence, or they can easily be perceived as a threat. Try and anticipate what the team experience might look like from the new staff member's point of view and seek feedback from the staff member to spot problems and to be able to offer reassurance. Being candid may be necessary to help them make sense of what they have experienced; if this is hard, given your responsibilities, then this is where a mentor can help (see below).

It is also worth remembering that informal contact with the team matters. This is not just about finding a place in the team; there is a lot to be learned, socially, from what happens around you. New members of staff need to be in a communal space where they can meet people, and see what is going on, not tucked away in an outbuilding. Also remember that personal space and comfort matter and help someone belong. Their own desk, phone, IT equipment and a parking space can help a lot. It should not be a case of 'last in, most disadvantaged'!

Provision of mentors

One way of supporting new staff members' induction is to provide them with a mentor. A mentor is a more experienced colleague who offers friendship and support as well as guidance, information, counsel and advice. This can take a lot of the weight off you and, if the mentor is in close contact or working alongside the 'mentee', and has the time to show the new person around and introduce him or her to others, it can be an excellent way of finding a way into a team. However, bear in mind this is skilled work and demands the right attitude, so be careful who you pick. Because mentoring is supportive and not a formal management role, sometimes people think it doesn't need to be planned. Whilst being available and listening are important, a mentor needs to be proactive and to be contributing to the induction plan. Mentors also need to be easy to contact and regular meetings are a must, as well as informal opportunities. Sometimes staff who have recently been through induction can be more useful than more experienced staff.

Involving the wider team

Most of the points we have discussed in exploring the involvement of your immediate team apply. Partners and co-providers in service provision should be as keen as you are to offer an effective induction; in fact it can be a great pleasure to meet a new colleague and show that person around. However, once again it is 'judgement call' time. They may not see the impor-tance of induction and so you may need to meet up with them, or ask a member of your team to work with them, to get them on board.

Alternatively, induction can be explored and planned with the network of service providers working as a team, so that it is a shared responsibility and experience, e.g. the local day services manager hosts your team member and introduces him or her to the team and service, community services, and local service user and carer organisations. It is worth bearing in mind that other service providers should want their staff to visit your team and gain an under-standing of your work as well, so arrangements and benefits can be reciprocal. This total team approach may well be the best way forward and can offer a wider resource base to draw on.

Integrating with organisational provision

Given the size of the task, organisational provision can be a huge help, taking a lot of the weight off you and the team. However, it cannot really compensate for helping someone gain local knowledge and there is also a danger of the personal issues being lost. Nevertheless, if you and your team recognise this, you can shape your activity to complement the corporate induction.

The secret of developing local provision that complements central provision is seeking feedback on the experience from the new staff member. This allows you to respond to gaps in what is offered or else to 'bespoke' it. That is, you may need to discuss the implications of a particular issue locally or help the staff member translate something so that it makes sense. So, for instance, if there is a corporate health and safety briefing (and there often is), check out how it went and what your new colleague got from it and explore local issues and implications for practice.

Central providers of induction programmes may involve you in their design and evaluation and ensure you are briefed on their programme. If they don't, find out about them and what is on offer, and discuss what they offer with your staff member, or get a member of the team to. After your colleague has attended the programme, discuss it with your new team member and give the central provider your perspectives on the effectiveness of the programme and how it could be improved. You could ask a team member to take lead responsibility for liaising with and integrating local with central provision.

Using other learning resources

There are a lot of learning resources that can be integrated into the induction process. Apart from national and local policy documents there are also learning packs produced by employing organisations as well as national bodies such as Skills for Care.

Do bear in mind we are discussing learning resources and there are issues around whether anyone has actually learnt anything; as seen in Section One, there are different levels of learn-ing. It is easy to 'throw' policy documents and learning packs at someone or say they can be found on the corporate website, but has the new staff member really learnt from them and incorporated them into practice or even looked at them? Staff really need an opportunity to discuss their thinking and the impact on their practice to develop a deeper approach. Again, involving colleagues is a good way to make policy and procedures come alive; for example, maybe ask someone to help the new staff member find a local policy on the intranet and then discuss with that person how it has impacted on the colleague's own work and pick up any questions your new staff member might have.

Developing local resources is another possibility. As suggested earlier, a team map of co-providers and partners can be invaluable but a resource file that contains brochures describing services that can be incorporated into care plans, application forms and even team members' comments and evaluations can be very useful. Libraries of useful journal articles and books can also be incredibly helpful to new colleagues, together with good examples of reports and letters.

ACTIVITY **10.2**

Induction packs

What would you include in a locally produced induction pack for new people joining your team? How would you make this pack flexible enough to meet the individual needs of workers and students in different roles?

However, while accepting that local resources can possibly be valuable, they also present a picture of your team. A resource library that is a mess and hopelessly out of date will not inspire anyone. So someone needs to take responsibility for not only creating it but managing it and updating it. The same applies to organisational policy and procedures which change over time. Unfortunately, it is not unusual for people to be given out-of-date policy documents or learning packs, because neither the people who originally produced them or anyone on the ground has checked them recently. There can be a lot to cover, and so this is another opportunity to encourage people in the team to contribute and take responsibility according to their special interests.

Another danger is overwhelming the new member of staff. The transition will be different depending on the individual. Some will be familiar with policy, practices and resources and will adjust quickly. Others will have more to learn. Learning styles and abilities will differ and so new staff members need to work at a pace that is right for them. Also, you will need to keep an eye on total volume. Determine the priorities and essentials, the 'must knows', then let them move beyond that according to needs and interests in the longer term.

A range of learning methods can make induction a more stimulating experience and can also ensure that the different learning styles and preferences of individual staff members have been responded to. Methods you might consider using are:

- coaching and one-to-one discussion;
- shadowing a colleague or colleagues;
- sitting in on planning meetings, reviews and conferences;
- visits and short placements;
- guided reading;

- distance learning;

- e-learning;

- taught components and programmes;

- dedicated and structured supervision sessions;

- mentoring by a colleague or colleagues;

- group work and learning sets.

Standards for induction

You will need to familiarise yourself with any national induction standards for your sector and you will find that assistance and guidance in planning and implementing induction and assessment tools, and guidance on assessment are readily available.

The ASYE programme is being implemented in a phased way from September 2012. Its aim is to ensure that NQSWs receive consistent support in their first year of practice so that they are able to become confident, competent professionals. ASYE assessment details were not fully established at the time of writing and so we recommend that you visit the websites of the College of Social Work (**www.collegeofsocialwork.org**) and Skills for Care (**www.skills forcare.org.uk**) for up-to-date information and guidance.

In the case of unqualified care workers who are being introduced to the essential values, skills and knowledge that will allow them to do their job, some centralised provision can be useful. There are now common national induction standards (**www.skillsforcare.org.uk/cis/**) or competences that these staff must be seen to meet and this can be very demanding on a manager who must carry out an initial assessment of need, plan the teaching and learning programme and assess competence. A taught programme that offers external assessment can be a great help as it provides a core around which you can build local work-based experiences. As the standards are linked to National Vocational Qualifications (NVQs), this also gives your staff member a good start in obtaining a qualification.

Probation as an introduction to appraisal

Most employers build in a probationary period as part of the contract of employment. Typically it is six months but it can be a few weeks or even a year. If a new staff member's conduct or performance is viewed as unsatisfactory by his or her manager during the probationary period then employment can be terminated, sometimes with a reduced period of notice. In effect the probationary period is a first appraisal that allows an early identification of performance problems and early termination.

Unfortunately the probationary period, which runs parallel with, and is integrated into, the induction process, is often not given the attention it deserves. This is a shame as it sets the scene for future appraisals influencing expectations and behaviours. The following points need to be considered.

- Make sure you and your new staff member are aware of the procedures and your responsibilities during the probationary period. Be aware that new staff members will be anxious about it and may not raise it themselves or be that proactive in managing it. It is an area where you need to take a lead, but sensitively and positively, whilst giving as much control as possible to the staff member.

- It is worth remembering that it is reciprocal. If it allows an employer to terminate a contract early, it also allows a staff member to leave early. It may pay you to make this explicit and ensure staff members have good opportunity to express and discuss anything they are unhappy with. This sets a good model for future appraisals, and it is an opportunity for both parties to consider performance.

- Be clear what criteria your staff member's performance will be judged against. Typically this could be the job description, the Professional Capabilities Framework (which will replace the National Occupational Standards), the Common Induction Standards or other relevant codes of practice.

- Be clear what evidence you will draw on in judging someone's performance. If you will be drawing on other colleagues' views, this should be transparent.

- Remember it is an opportunity to give someone positive feedback on performance as well as identify problems. Try and keep feedback balanced and evidenced and make sure new staff members are aware and take credit for their strengths and achievements. It is no good appreciating someone's work but then not telling that person.

- Be clear on when you will meet, how discussion will be recorded, how the final report will be written and when the new staff member will receive written confirmation of successful completion or otherwise.

- There should be no surprises. Your staff member should receive clear feedback on progress or any problems. Concerns should be raised early and the staff member should be given the opportunity to discuss them. The issue and the discussion should be recorded and the record included in the final report. Remind new staff to raise concerns they might have and check that they think they are getting the support they need.

- If you or your staff member are identifying performance problems and learning needs, the induction process needs to be shaped to respond. This is how the two processes are integrated. Your staff member may need help using any of the teaching and learning methods we have identified above. Once the person has received support and guidance, he or she should be reassessed.

- If someone hasn't yet demonstrated competence the probationary period can be extended to allow that person to do so. You will need to consult with personnel/HR and be sure you can clearly identify the areas of performance the individual still needs to demonstrate competence in. It may be that the new colleague simply hasn't had time to do this yet; for instance, sickness can be a problem. However, if you do not think the person can success-fully demonstrate competence or there is a failing in professional conduct, postponing doing something is unhelpful.

- If someone's performance is so unsatisfactory or you have concerns about professional conduct, you do not have to wait until the end of the probationary period before dismissing that person – but do seek advice from personnel/HR.

- If your opinion is that someone has not successfully completed the probationary period you need to follow dismissal procedures. These usually consist of notice in writing, a meeting to discuss the outcome supported by a friend, and right to appeal. Ensure you take advice from personnel/HR.

- If someone has successfully completed the probationary period it offers a useful end point to induction. Take the opportunity to link it into the appraisal system by perhaps establishing objectives for the next six months and also determining development needs that either you or the staff member have identified. Make sure the individual is clear about staff development and appraisal processes and responsibilities.

FURTHER READING

Bradley, G. (2008) The induction of newly appointed social workers: some implications for social work educators. *Social Work Education,* 27(4): 349–365.

Coulsted, V., Mullender, A., Jones, D.N. and Thompson, N. (2006) *Management in Social Work.* Basingstoke: Macmillan.

Walker, J., Crawford, K. and Parker, J. (2008) *Practice Education in Social Work.* Exeter: Learning Matters.

Chapter 11
Appraisal

In many organisations personal development planning and continuing professional development (CPD) are linked with appraisal and directed towards improving performance. This chapter therefore considers appraisal as a learning tool as well as a way to review the performance and potential of staff.

The Advisory, Conciliation and Arbitration Service (ACAS) suggests that:

> *Appraisals regularly record an assessment of an employee's performance, potential and development needs. The appraisal is an opportunity to take an overall view of work content, loads and volumes, to look back on what has been achieved during the reporting period and agree objectives for the next.*

> (ACAS, 2001)

When focusing on the task the appraisal process seems a relatively simple process (Figure 11.1).

However, this apparent simplicity masks a complexity that readily generates problems in practice. Data collection is often neglected or lacking in method. At best, organisations use 360-degree feedback (Armstrong, 2006), but at worst the effectiveness of the whole process is dependent on a manager's often prejudiced perceptions. However, in health and social care regular supervision should mean that a supervising manager has a very rich picture of someone's practice, so a formal annual appraisal can draw on performance management throughout the year.

Analysis of performance is dependent on the quality of the data collected and the quality of the analysis. A range of benchmarks or comparators is commonly used in organisations to help managers in making judgements:

- competencies or standards of performance;
- organisational strategy or objectives;
- individually agreed objectives;
- delegated projects;
- rating system linked to performance pay levels;
- organisational performance measures;
- job specification.

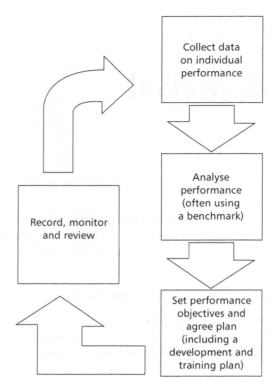

Figure 11.1 Appraisal process.

Codes of practice and professional values offer other points of reference and you may find you draw on a range of comparators. As mentioned earlier, the Professional Capabilities Framework (PCF) is based on the stages of a social worker's career from the first year of practice and outlines the expectations at each stage. It is envisaged that it will be used by employers to agree pay and grading structures as it will provide outcome statements for different levels. It can also be incorporated into an employer's appraisal systems. In parallel with this, the Health and Care Professions Council is developing the standards of proficiency for social workers that will be the basis for registration as a social worker and these will link with the PCF.

However, capabilities or standards only assist. Judging performance is complex because practice is complex. In fact, it could be argued that evaluating performance is the most demanding of professional activities. Sets of competencies and the new PCF can help, but in reality practice cannot be that clearly defined and demands considerable professional judgement. For instance, in supervision managers will not usually refer to standards in determining whether practice is satisfactory but will have a mental model they draw on. Standards, perhaps, only offer a common language in which performance can be expressed.

Recording performance objectives and improvement and development plans should be relatively straightforward, but in reality objectives and improvement plans are often unclear and, crucially, the document may never be referred to again until the next annual appraisal is due. Often organisations judge the effectiveness of their appraisal system by the number completed, with no regard given to their quality. These problems, that stem partly from a very difficult task, mean that in our experience managers and staff very often hate appraisal and view it as waste of time. In fact, it might be hard to find anyone who values it. In terms of enabling others it is therefore perhaps your biggest challenge.

Why do we all hate appraisal?

As suggested above, it is partly because it is hard. McGregor drew attention back in the 1950s to how unpopular appraisal is in the private sector and also pointed out how damaging appraisal is, putting it down to managers not liking to stand in judgement over others (McGregor, 1957). But there is a bit more to it than that, and he identified the essence of the problem areas by suggesting that a manager's values and attitudes towards staff were essential features of leadership. He identified two mindsets as 'theory X' and 'theory Y'.

Theory X: authoritarian

- People dislike work and will avoid it if they can.

- Staff must be coerced, controlled, directed or threatened with punishment in order to get them to achieve organisational objectives.

- People prefer to be directed and seek to avoid responsibility; they are unambitious and want security above all else.

Theory Y: participative

- Work is as natural as play and rest.

- People will exercise self-control and self-direction in the pursuit of organisational objectives, without external control or the threat of punishment being necessary.

- Staff will accept and seek responsibility.

- People will readily use imagination, ingenuity and creativity in solving organisational problems.

- The true potential of people is not utilised in organisations.

(Based on McGregor, 2005)

McGregor (2005) suggests that managers with a theory X attitude create theory X behaviours in their staff by their controlling approach, whereas theory Y thinking and approaches generate theory Y behaviours. If we apply this to appraisal, it becomes apparent why appraisal is such a problem. Appraisal was introduced to public services as part of the 'New Public Sector Management' that sought to introduce business practices and improve efficiency and effectiveness (Flynn, 2002). It conflicted with the previous culture, where managing performance was mainly the concern of the individual professional. Appraisal systems are often designed corporately so they don't necessarily fit a particular service; they are centrally imposed and compulsory. They can also be the basis for people being disciplined or dismissed or not promoted. They are therefore the point where all the negatives of organisational power come together and are made explicit, when often in our everyday work they are hidden.

In sum, appraisal is 'in your face' theory X management and staff slip quickly into theory X mode in response, being appraised reluctantly and often just going through the motions. If managers don't like judging and find it hard, staff don't like being judged either and find it equally hard. So what is to be done? What does theory Y appraisal look like and can it be achieved? McGregor (1957) suggests a shift away from the concept of appraisal as something that is done to you, towards the idea of analysis, with the individual taking responsibility and control of the process, and focusing on development and improvement in the future rather than looking to the past.

Engaging staff in appraisal

There is no point in pretending this is going to be easy. Creating enabling appraisal is very much a case of 'flying against the wind' for the reasons given above. Part of the struggle is trying to work against the all-too-common 'top-down' approach of organisations to appraisal, and their negative history, so you will find yourself trying to change organisational culture. One way to do this is to try and mobilise your community of practice (see Chapter 5). What part does appraisal play in a community of practice? One answer is that appraisal has no part to play in a community practice at all, as the focus should be on team achievement. However, individual attention can also be seen as an important part of a community of practice (Gray *et al.*, 2010b) and this accords with Adair's (1983) action-centred leadership that sees a team leader's responsibilities as needing to be focused on developing the team and developing the individual in order to achieve the task (Figure 11.2).

Regular team meetings and a team development agenda need to run alongside leading and managing individuals through supervision and CPD.

The areas of overlap in Figure 11.2 are significant because activities that integrate the three dimensions lie in those spaces, and are more likely to be effective. For instance, team meetings to explore appraisal will draw on team resources and energies and, in allowing a discussion of some of the issues raised in this chapter, may foster a more positive attitude. Also, in a community of practice individual appraisal needs to value contributing to the team with opportunity for team review of team performance to complement individual appraisal.

Reframing appraisal can also be useful and can be part of the team agenda. If it has been mishandled in many organisations it could be seen as an important right for employees as a member of an organisation and a response to personal needs. This means emphasising some aspects of appraisal that are too easily lost. For instance, it provides the opportunity to identify service or organisational problems that are affecting the quality of a professional practice and bring improvement, i.e. there should be two-way traffic. Yet this is the part of appraisal that is often most neglected (Mullins, 2007). The rights met for a professional through appraisal might look something like this:

- the right to contribute to and formally agree an evaluation of my performance with my manager that identifies my achievements and for this to be recorded;
- the right to transparent judgements about my performance to ensure fairness in gradings, promotions and references, including the right to disagree and have the disagreement formally recorded;

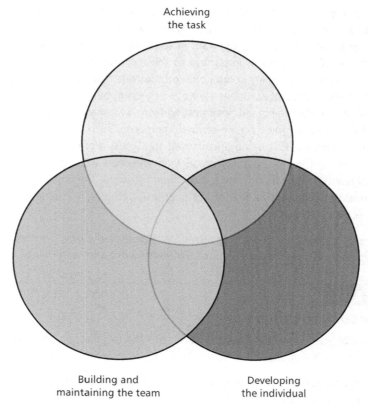

Achieving
the task

Building and
maintaining the team

Developing
the individual

Figure 11.2 What a leader has to do (Adair 1983: 44).

- the right to have performance problems promptly and clearly identified and to be supported in resolving them;
- the right to have clear, agreed objectives for improving my practice;
- the right to a personal development plan supported and resourced by my manager so that my practice continuously improves;
- the right to a fair workload that does not undermine my health and well-being;
- the right to identify organisational problems that are undermining my practice and for them to be responded to;
- the right to explore how I am led, managed and supported to plan for improvement;
- the right to a career plan that allows me to reach my potential as a professional and experience a high-quality working experience that maximises my health and well-being.

If reframing appraisal with the team is important, this needs to be translated into practice through your leadership. Appraisal does need to give time and attention to identifying organisational problems that are undermining practice and you will need to respond to them once they have been identified. Career planning is also too often neglected entirely, and workload management, combined with an exploration of the quality of working experience, is deserving of particular attention. This can help develop a positive 'psychological contract' (Armstrong, 2006).

The psychological contract is the hidden contract between your staff member and the wider organisation, and it is far more important than the formal organisational contract. It encompasses all the things that are important in someone's working life, including what may seem trivial to someone else but is important to the staff member. A positive psychological contract means that employees are committed and motivated. A negative one can mean they are disillusioned and unmotivated, or even leave. So checking out in appraisal what people are enjoying, or what is undermining and demotivating them, and then responding where you can, is very important. As seen earlier, person-centred approaches such as these enable meaningful and appropriate learning. Just being encouraged to express dissatisfaction and then being listened to can, in itself, make a big difference. Team members will also know there are some organisational realities you cannot change but if you recognise the impact on them they can feel a lot more appreciated. The leadership people experience is crucial here and can be essential to people's well-being.

There is currently a welcome interest in improving workplace well-being. For more information, visit the well-being website at **www.dwp.gov.uk/health-work-and-well-being/**.

ACTIVITY 11.1

Your approach to appraisal

How do you approach appraisal? Are you rolling with the negative aspects and approaching appraisal as a theory X manager or are you a theory Y appraiser?

What might you try in order to engage your staff more effectively in appraisal? What could you do to improve your own appraisal?

Career planning

It is worth considering the part career development plays in your appraisal practice. Putting appraisal in the wider context of career planning can make a big difference to its quality, i.e. exploring what someone wants to achieve in his or her career and helping that person reach for it. Apart from benefiting the individual this also benefits the service.

If career development is important and if it is to be focused on well-being, it is worth considering a 'softer' approach that contrasts with the more technocratic world of management standards, processes and plans. Joy-Mathews *et al.* (2004: 141) developed a useful way of thinking about this. They contrast the conventional formula for a good objective SMART, i.e. specific, measurable, actionable, realistic and time-bound, with SPICE:

- spiritual;
- physical;
- intellectual;
- career;
- emotional.

They suggest that it is important to approach CPD and career planning as a whole person and in a balanced way, and this demands giving attention to aspects of self that the organisation does not necessarily respond to. So, beyond specific learning or developmental objectives, people should have goals that will help them meet not just career ambitions but spiritual, physical, intellectual and emotional needs.

Another way to express this is to suggest that it is important that people reach out for what makes them happy. You may find it useful to visit the work of Csikszentmihalyi (1988, 1990, 2008), who is a positive psychologist who has researched what gives people happiness; he points out how important it is that work is meaningful and that pleasure can be taken from the process as well as the outcomes.

Working with your team members can help them think back over work experiences and identify posts, projects and roles that have given them particular satisfaction or in which they have been successful and proud of the achievement. Encourage them to identify skills that they are proud of, challenges they thrive on, work that has engaged and motivated them and also activities or responsibilities to avoid. There are some fundamental value issues here about what people want to achieve in their lives, and although this can raise questions about work–life balance, it is worth remembering that eight hours a day, five days a week of their lives are spent with you. Do bear in mind, however, that people's career ambitions are different and can vary over time. Being true to one's values, work–life balance, and challenge and advancement can be weighted differently by different people, and this weighting can change as someone's career progresses, following quite different patterns (Mainiero and Sullivan, 2005).

If it is important that your career planning has this added personal depth, there are still some practical things that appraisees can do to help set career goals and find direction.

Get advice

Human resources or personnel departments as well as professional bodies may be able to offer advice and guidance on career prospects and pathways. Succession planning is figuring more in public service thinking so you may find these people helpful. Alternatively, you can help the appraisee yourself, working from your career experience. Another option is approaching people who are in the sort of posts the appraisee might be interested in and suggest they ask them:

- What attracted them to their job?

- What do they think was key to them getting it?

- What have been the challenges for them?

- What have they found most enjoyable?

- What have they not enjoyed?

- What do they see as their next step?

- What would they advise someone to do if they are aiming for a similar appointment?

If possible, shadowing someone for a day or sitting in on some key events can be useful. For instance, if the appraisee wants to follow a management pathway, sitting in on some strategy or senior team meetings could help.

Mentoring

What can really be valuable is if someone in a post or role they are interested in will agree to be the appraisee's mentor (see Chapter 8).

Research opportunities

Suggest the appraisee scans advertised posts, gets the job descriptions and person specifications and does a gap analysis against his or her current experience, skills and knowledge. Perhaps also explore the training and development provision that is offered to people in the post. When benchmarking practice, look at higher levels than the appraisee's current post demands. There are also employment agencies and consultants who offer career guidance.

Plan

Help appraisees set career goals, and include activities that will help them meet them in their development plan. They may need a short- and long-term plan and it might be an idea to build in some contingency and alternative pathways or options. If you can persuade your organisation to take on these longer-term development needs as part of a succession planning initiative, then they will be in an even better position.

Delegate

Delegate some responsibilities or a development that would not normally be in your remit but will allow appraisees to demonstrate skills or experience an aspect of the role they might be interested in.

Becoming a proactive appraiser

Even though it is a good tactic to build back in the elements that appraisal currently tends to leave out, a lot can still come down to you and your attitude and behaviour. For instance, it isn't uncommon for managers to leave all the preparation to the staff member, with that individual drafting a review of his or her activities and achievements and the manager simply endorsing them. To be effective you need to identify achievements and any difficulties. This means there should be 'no surprises' when it comes to the appraisal; but crucially, if you review your records you should be able to provide a clear view on someone's performance. It makes a big difference if you are seen to have been proactive, and this is an opportunity to remind people of what they have achieved and to thank them. Again, we see the principles of person-centred leading and enabling practice here. If you have no viewpoint it is almost disrespectful, and what is an opportunity for effective leadership becomes an empty ritual.

In giving feedback make sure you emphasise the positives. Keep objectives for improvement focused and achievable, and support the appraisee in the long term, e.g. with developmental opportunities and coaching and discussion in supervision. This is also an opportunity to get feedback on your performance as manager and supervisor. Work to the same principle and seek feedback (e.g. in supervision sessions) and pull points together for the appraisal. Ask the appraisee as part of the appraisal to comment directly on your performance and what you could do better. This is bound to be uncomfortable but the most likely result is that both you and your staff member will say the positive things and show the appreciation that very often isn't said until the leaving party when either you or the appraisee are saying goodbye!

ACTIVITY **11.2**

Reflecting on your appraisal practice

What can you do personally to make appraisal more rewarding for both you and your staff?

FURTHER READING

View Csikszentmihalyi on YouTube. Available from: http://uk.youtube.com/watch?v=fXIeFJCqsPs

Health Work Wellbeing website. Department for Work and Pensions. Available from: http://www.dwp.gov.uk/health-work-and-well-being/

Joy-Mathews, J., Megginson, D. and Surtees, M. (2004) *Human Resource Development*. London: Kogan Page.

McGregor, D. (2005) *The Human Side of Enterprise*. New York: McGraw-Hill.

Chapter 12

Service user and carer involvement

This chapter cannot hope to do justice to the wealth of advice, themes and messages in this area and so the aim is to try and highlight a few general points before focusing on aspects of service users' and carers' involvement in facilitating work-based learning and development. From service users' point of view, two key points of learning have been identified by user groups for social work training/education – understanding what a carer and/or service user's life is like, and the overall significance of the quality of the relationship between them and social workers (DoH, 2002a).

Carers and people who use services have a critical role in facilitating learning and development in social care. Participation by individuals and groups can be a very powerful and effective means for improving social care outcomes and the processes of service delivery. Involving the public, carers and people who use social care services in development initiatives in service design and delivery, research, and in the education of practitioners has been increasingly promoted in recent government policies in the UK, and is high on the agenda of the regulatory bodies (DoH, 2002b, 2006; Lowes and Hullatt, 2005; SWRB, 2010). In recent years in Britain, service user and carer participation within social service planning, delivery, education and research has developed at a rapid pace, so that some say we have *entered a new era – that of the empowered service user* (Carey, 2009: 180). A report developed by service users and carers and commissioned by the Social Care Institute for Excellence (Sadd, 2011) provides evidence of the value of sustaining and improving involvement in the selection, teaching and assessment of student social workers, and in the design and evaluation of social work degrees.

Such involvement and participation can be viewed as *one of the essential cogs that keep the wheel of planning, delivering and evaluating social care policies and resources running* (Hafford-Letchfield *et al.*, 2008: 88) because user-centred practice/services (where a focus is placed on users and their priorities) is a key enabler of change. Of course, the very terms used to identify the people involved, such as 'service user' and 'carer', can be stigmatising and excluding to some (Hefferman, 2006). We use these terms with the proviso that they are not intended to convey any reductive or discriminatory connotations and we realise that there are distinctions between the two groups. There is no single agreed definition of involvement either (Moriarty *et al.*, 2007) and a multitude of terms can be found in the literature, which in some ways can show the level and type of involvement concerned:

- participation;
- engagement;

- consultation;

- inclusion;

- access;

- representation.

We will primarily use 'involvement' as a catch-all term, although others may also be used within the chapter.

There is a large amount of information, materials, research and case examples available through organisations such as Social Care Institute for Excellence (SCIE) and Social Work Education Participation (SWEP) which aim to make such involvement and participation in formal social work education and in service development meaningful and effective (see further reading on page 98 for details).

Leadership role

In leading and enabling learning in the workplace there is also a role to play in embedding

> *user and carer participation, both formally and informally into the fabric of learning and development . . . using a variety of organisational and strategic frameworks.*

> (Hafford-Letchfield *et al.*, 2008: 77)

The number of ways in which involvement in workplace learning can take place is wide-ranging, e.g. involvement in training events, in service development events, in the decision-making processes/governance regarding training or service development events, and/or as an everyday, proactive involvement in a relationship with a social worker.

> *User participation has to encompass a whole spectrum of learning, from awareness, reflection and work-based learning to active involvement in strategic planning and service delivery.*

> (Hafford-Letchfield *et al.*, 2008: 95)

Think about the ways in which your organisation has involved carers and people who use services in learning/development events or initiatives, and how your commitment is needed to express the importance of any involvement to others, maintain its momentum and make things happen in the best way.

General models

Hanley *et al.* (2003) suggest a model which offers three levels of involvement – consultation, collaboration and user control. Consultation can be seen as asking carers and service users about their views on a particular issue, policy or approach. Collaboration may be seen as a more active ongoing partnership or alliance with carers and service users, who may join a group or committee. User-controlled involvement usually signifies that the locus of power is with the service users and carers. However, it does not necessarily mean that they under-take every stage of any project or that professionals are totally excluded. Involvement can be an organic process which develops and grows through these stages within a supportive partnership.

More recently, a *whole systems approach* (Wright *et al.,* 2006) has been advocated based on four key elements pictured as parts of a jigsaw to show their interaction and dependence on each other (Moriarty *et al.,* 2007):

1. develop a *culture* – this is the ethos of the organisation shared by all staff and service users;

2. develop a *structure* – the planning, development and resourcing of involvement;

3. develop effective *practice* – the ways of working, methods for involvement, skills and knowledge;

4. develop effective *review* systems – the monitoring and evaluation systems to evidence involvement.

The idea is for you to put the different pieces of the puzzle together in ways that can support your team or organisation at different points in their journey towards involving people.

General issues

Meaningful service user involvement can be challenging (Duffy, 2008) but this should not produce a negative association. Many potential barriers can be overcome with foresight, understanding and a will to address them. The potential barriers from a service user's perspective are explained by Tyler (2006), e.g. transport, child care or adult care costs, payments that don't interfere with benefits, jargon use, intimidating meetings, physical access. Hafford-Letchfield *et al.* (2008) look at other issues that can impact on the effectiveness of any involvement, including the difficulty of attaining shared outcomes, values and attitudes, and clear lines of accountability. The more practical issues will be easier to overcome than those which are culturally embedded.

Involvement that is more than tokenistic requires commitment and resources – for you to build up trust and interpersonal relationships, to negotiate aims and responsibilities, and to ensure that all concerned possess the skills needed for the task. Levels of commitment and resourcing will be set according to the organisational view of working from a user or person-centred perspective, and so your organisational culture will be of vital consequence in defining how meaningful and appropriate any involvement process will be. A will and a desire to involve people in a meaningful way has to be firmly entrenched within the whole of the service, otherwise political agendas, managerialist cultures and cost-effective bureaucracies can create insurmountable problems.

Service users and carers are a very mixed group of people and so you will need to be aware of and take into account all the issues that may affect their involvement, e.g. past history, level of disability or awareness, experience of working with organisations. Service users should have the opportunity to participate in ways that suit them – there needs to be variety and flexibility of approaches and methods. This depends, in turn, on you getting to know them in order to get the best kind of response, and finding creative ways together not only to deal with the practical things that may hinder participation (e.g. provision of signers, interpreters, access issues, support workers), but also to find out what people think without leading or prompting them too much.

To avoid a tick-box approach to involvement, i.e. just saying 'yes, we've listened' or making some token gesture representation, a leader needs to enable the type of engagement that ensures people feel they have a stake in the services which are supposedly there for their benefit. So this is not about service users waiting to be asked but you enabling them to voice views and opinions about what should change or develop in their own time and in their own way.

Again, it is the culture in which these structures and practices are embedded that will be the critical element for whether and how well this is achieved; and as a leader or enabler you should at least have some opportunity to create an environment that is person-centred. This link to learning cultures is significant and, indeed, user involvement has itself been identified as a key to change.

> *Cultural change and service user involvement are inherently linked. Improving the practice around user involvement at all levels – which is cultural change in itself – is the key to improving change in all other aspects of service provision.*

(Shaping Our Lives, 2007: 4)

This is an interesting point. As noted earlier, a true learning organisation, and any team where a learning culture is embedded, would have already adopted an inclusive approach to participation where people (staff and service users) have a natural right to be involved in planning and decision making at everyday and more strategic levels (Robson *et al.*, 2008). However, if such a culture is not present and staff are not consulted and involved in meaningful and empowering ways, how can you ensure it happens for service users and carers? Ultimately, meaningful involvement is about value and respect being shown to people as true allies, with managers and leaders actively acknowledging and fully addressing the power issues, hopefully at both strategic and practice levels, but always modelling and generating their own positive and inclusive culture.

ACTIVITY 12.1

Benefits and barriers to involvement

List the benefits, tensions or barriers associated with this topic which have become apparent in your organisation, or could potentially become apparent. Identify which attitudes lead to service users being excluded. Are these due to cultures, structures, practices or something else? Can they be overcome?

Map how and where involvement occurs now (or not); identify any 'champions' and also the areas that need improvement.

Formalised involvement in workplace learning

Carers and service users, and their organisations, can contribute to practice learning by being involved in continuing professional development or post-qualifying as well as qualifying training or formal education. This can require systematic, explicit and formalised processes, but it doesn't have to be restricted to direct teaching or group-work; some may prefer to meet learners informally on a one-to-one basis or allow visits at home.

Opportunities for involvement in learning

- materials for use in individual study;

- group work, e.g. videos of interviews or role plays;

- direct input into seminars or workshops;

- shadowing;

- observations;

- interviews;

- role plays;

- projects;

- visits.

Involvement in training and learning depends on your own and other practitioners' commitment to users taking part, a willingness to accompany and support users where appropriate or necessary, and for everyone to be trained to know how to involve service users (CCNAP, 2001). Involvement starts at the beginning to define priorities, set and monitor standards, clear expectations and any contracts. There are a number of things to think about and plan for, and you will need to work with people well in advance of any involvement. For example, users and carers each have a different experience of services and they may well have their own agendas. Negotiation may need to establish common ground and boundaries for representation. There is a real need to be realistic about timescales and what can be achieved; it is better to do something small and well, rather than be overly optimistic and achieve a poor outcome.

There should be some creative group thinking about how to achieve appropriate learning and also assessment opportunities whilst establishing trust and mutual respect together.

Opportunities for learning

- Work alongside service users in user-controlled organisations, services (e.g. independent living centres) or other networks.

- Learners shadow or follow service users, carers and their families for substantial periods of time.

- Learners interview service users and carers, who in turn provide a commentary on their performance that can be fed into assessment.

- Questionnaires are produced with service users to help them provide feedback on their involvement with a student – start from the service user perspective, not core competencies.

- Preparation materials are developed and meetings set up for service users to facilitate their involvement in the feedback process.

- Develop a training programme for service users interested in developing their expertise as trainers and educators.

- Create a video together for use as a teaching tool – being at the receiving end of social workers' communication skills.

- Develop user-led assessment. Build a set of criteria to assess the value base of students and the processes through which they engage with, and serve, service users and carers – an *experiential assessment framework* (Advocacy in Action, 2006).

- Establish a network of service users in a local region.

Assessment opportunities: practicalities to be addressed

- Who makes the assessment, when, how and to whom?

- What is being assessed: knowledge, skills, values? Advocacy in Action (2006: 339) suggests that it is *the process of service delivery, its underlying values and power relationships that people on the receiving end are best placed to experience and assess*, and has developed its own experiential assessment framework for this.

- Is assessment to be formative (feedback only) or summative (involving marks or measurement)?

- Is the feedback given directly to the learner or collated by someone else, e.g. a practice assessor?

- What weight will be attached to the service users' and carers' assessments of learners' work or practice, as they may differ from others' assessment decisions?

- Will there be participation in practice assessment panels?

- Be clear about the consequences of doing this – is the organisation/student/staff member prepared to make changes? Is there a planned opportunity to reflect and work through responses to feedback?

Support for formal involvement in workplace learning

Facilitating the workplace learning of new and established staff and placement students is not an easy job and can make some people doubt their personal capacities. Carers and service users should not be expected to participate without access to training and support to develop their skills and confidence if they require it.

Not everyone is suited to the role, e.g. those with closed tunnel vision about their own cause or illness, or those only interested in relaying negative experiences and not being sufficiently broad-minded. Also, any training cannot prepare carers and service users for the unexpected. Some students or practitioners will feel that they know all about antidiscriminatory practice and equality and don't need to hear it from anyone else. Service users and carers could co-train, but at the very least it is vital for peer support to have been set up in advance to help deal with problematic students and/or staff. However, gaining confidence and expertise as educators can enable service users to find effective strategies so that they can use their personal knowledge and ideas effectively with others. The amount, level and range of training required are becoming more truly recognised, as is the need to maintain such involvement. Some may want training and support to gain a recognised qualification and accreditation for their contributions.

Hastings (2000) asserts that training should ideally be delivered to carers and service users by their peers, since this will in itself prove empowering and encouraging, and will challenge the unequal user–professional power dynamic. He identifies content areas of training areas as:

- personal development of self-confidence;

- assertiveness and communication;

- training in practical skills, such as how to design and facilitate training workshops;

- learning how to participate on committees;

- learning how to plan and deliver material;

- how to draw upon subjective experience and apply it in generally useful forms.

Day-to-day involvement in everyday decision making about services

Reflective practitioners should:

- understand a carer's or service user's life and needs;

- be aware of how their relationship and the service provision is perceived from the service user's perspective;

- involve that person as much as possible in decisions around their service provision.

In effect, service users' and carers' voices within the practice relationship should enhance this understanding, awareness and involvement, as well as the quality of the service.

> *Connecting users into the process of reflection and engagement with practice is at the heart of building the confidence, empathy, expertise and vision of staff, while also improving social care outcomes.*

(Hafford-Letchfield *et al.*, 2008: 89)

As we know, effectiveness in involving people comes from approach and attitude as well as technique, i.e. it's not just about what is done, it's also about how it's done. Leading and enabling others means having an awareness and understanding of the attitudes and approaches staff may be taking to their involvement with service users and carers. There may be an undercurrent of feeling that says 'we know what's good for you' amongst management and practitioners, with the notion that it is a professional responsibility to make the decisions and put services in place. Of course, professionals are trained and recruited to be experts with specialist knowledge and skills to make judgements about the best interests of their clients. Involvement of service users in everyday decision making about their services (an everyday participation approach) blurs the boundaries between roles because it shares this responsibility, which can be seen as a challenge to a professional role. It can also be seen that, although students and social workers are primed with politically correct thinking about carers and service users, the full complexity of the issue may not be understood. Applying labels and seeing people as 'other' can occur insidiously in the managerialist cultures found in many highly pressurised workplaces. Taylor and White (2006) show how easy it is for us to make quick moral judgements and apply group norms and understandings which immediately categorise people.

For many practitioners and organisations, though, there is no distinction between service delivery and participation of the service user. Involvement is part and parcel of everyday work, services, activities, relationships and events. Service users are made to feel valued and to develop the confidence to take part in decision making about services by being placed at the centre of the process, forming a proactive relationship between them (individually and collectively), the service, and, in particular, the staff. This everyday participation is the bedrock of involvement in all aspects of services, i.e. immediate needs as well as service development, management and governance. Such a genuine and positive approach that respects, values and also actively seeks the expertise service users contribute to this relationship means the service is more likely to be centred on their needs and priorities at that time (CCNAP, 2001).

Supporting reflective practice

Because so much work-based learning takes place through informal and experiential ways, the more that can be viewed through a service user's or carer's perspective, the more learning and development will take place. Encouraging and enabling an everyday participation approach with staff is about developing a particular type of learning culture – one where there is an appreciation of equality and of users supporting reflective practice. Such appreciation would also feed into and be enhanced by a community of practice.

Hafford-Letchfield *et al.* (2008: 90) suggest *establishing mechanisms for users to provide group supervision sessions, non-managerial support, mentoring and opportunities to explore the material contained within reflective diaries or learning journals.* They also suggest creating a safe space for exploring any fears associated with the idea of involving users in supporting reflective practice. (Service users would clearly need to be fully respecting confidentiality and not working with individuals or teams involved in their care.) They say there is much to learn from *exploring the perceived barriers and power dynamics associated with users facilitating reflective learning as there will be from actually reflecting on practice* (Hafford-Letchfield *et al.,* 2008: 91).

This is a recent and relatively unexplored area of service user involvement and of work-based learning and development too. We suggest that you seek further guidance to support you in any new endeavours in this area.

ACTIVITY **12.2**

Everyday involvement

Are service users/carers involved in everyday decision making in your organisation? When and how? Is this something that can be improved?

How do you feel about being mentored or supported by a service user? Does this shift in roles seem threatening or uncomfortable? As a barrier to learning, how could these feelings be approached?

Evaluation issues

Evaluation is concerned with making an assessment or judgement about the value and efficacy of any involvement. Although we are very restricted in the amount of space we can devote to the topic here, it is nonetheless a fundamental element and must not be ignored. In brief, you should make it part of an ongoing process, undertaken as part of interim monitoring and feedback procedures, as well as at the end. Hafford-Letchfield *et al.* (2008) note that evaluation should cover outcomes, limitations, resource implications and challenges. They also suggest that, when undertaken within a culture of learning, service users will be engaged directly in analysing findings and generating ideas for new ways of working as part of the evaluation process. It is especially important to think about how any feedback from the evaluation of formal training run by carers or service users will be handled. The impact can be profound because the training material is likely to be deeply personal. Again, the reader is directed to the SCIE and SWEP resources (see further reading, below) for a full range of ideas and materials.

The future

There is a requirement to acknowledge and incorporate the changing role of carers and service users from passive recipient to active partner and the associated changing social worker role as well. As partnership and collaboration are put centre-stage by government policy and rhetoric, leaders and managers need to be equipped to respond to the needs and wishes of carers and service users, and fully appreciate the range of ways in which they can engage in instilling change through facilitating learning and development.

Beresford and Boxall (2012) most recently argue that collective and organisational, as opposed to isolated, involvement of service users in social work education, research and practice is likely to be more effective in getting these perspectives heard, and for this knowledge not to be dominated or distorted by traditional or medicalised understandings.

Whether individual or collective, though, the role of the leader or enabler is to ensure that involvement in learning is genuine and meaningful (Robson *et al.*, 2008).

Branfield, F., Beresford, P. and Levin, E. (2007) *Common Aims: A strategy to support service user involvement in social work education*. Social Work Education Position Paper 07. London: SCIE.

Carey, M. (2009) Happy shopper? The problem with service user and carer participation. *British Journal of Social Work*, 39(1): 179–188.

SCIE (2012) *Towards Co-production: Taking participation to the next level*. Workforce Development Report 53. London: SCIE.

SCIE's participation resources address how practitioners and managers can initiate and sustain the participation of people who use services. See www.scie.org.uk/topic/keyissues/participation

Social Work Education Participation (SWEP): www.socialworkeducation.org.uk. The aim of this website is to share good practice around the participation of service users and carers in social work education. It has been developed by an alliance of the Social Care Institute for Excellence (SCIE), Shaping Our Lives, the University of Sussex and a steering group of service users and carers.

Chapter 13
Case reviews

In this chapter we explore how you can enable others to learn through case reviews. We consider how case reviews can be used internally and in multi-agency contexts to ensure that organisations involved in working with vulnerable children and adults get better at learning from experience by monitoring, critically evaluating and adapting their practice. In her final report, Munro (2011) highlighted the role of case reviews in ensuring that professionals are equipped with the skills to exercise judgement and take a more service user-centred approach to their practice. Crucially, the essence of a systems approach is that all the people and systems that interact together to create the user's experience of the service are taken into account. This provides a deeper analysis and is a valuable way of exploring and improving service quality. Munro suggested that the regular review of cases should become the norm and not just something that is done when things have gone wrong. In this chapter we will focus specifically on the systems approach to case reviews developed by the Social Care Institute for Excellence (Fish and Munro, 2008) and recommended by Munro (2011).

We begin this chapter by looking at serious case reviews and explore ways in which the outcomes of such reviews can be used to identify changes that are required to improve practice and minimise risk. We will then move on to explore how some of the methods and approaches used in serious case reviews can be adapted and used on a more regular basis within the workplace to support learning and enhance professional practice.

What is a serious case review?

Serious case reviews are convened when a child or a vulnerable adult dies or is seriously injured and there is a suspicion that abuse or neglect has played a role in the outcome. When such a tragic incident occurs, a number of investigations are triggered to establish what has happened and who is to blame. This normally includes enquiries by the police and the coroner's court as well as internal reviews by organisations that have been involved with the victim or victims. Serious case reviews are undertaken in addition to these other investigations; they are not disciplinary or criminal proceedings and do not set out to apportion blame to individuals. The purpose of the review is to:

- establish if there are lessons to be learned in situations where a number of agencies and professionals were working together in a safeguarding role;
- identify what the lessons are and how they will be acted on to improve practice;
- improve local interagency working;

- review procedures and make recommendations for improvements;

- prepare or commission a report that brings together the findings of individual agencies, identifying key learning points and recommendations.

Why a systems approach?

The systems approach to case reviews was first seen in the aviation industry where it was used to investigate crashes and near misses. It has since been adopted by other high-risk sectors such as health and social care, where it is primarily used as a method for reviewing cases where something has gone wrong. The approach is based on the premise that professionals operate within a system and that their performance in any situation is a result not only of their own skills and knowledge but also of the context in which they are working.

The following simple (and deliberately non-social work) example helps to illustrate how different investigations are used for different purposes and why it is important to take a systems approach to case review.

Jack has a two-year-old car which is very reliable and is his pride and joy. He has held a clean driving licence for 20 years and believes, with some justification, that he is a good driver. Although he enjoys driving fast when it is safe and legal to do so, he normally tries to keep within the legal speed limit. Shortly after a service Jack's car developed an intermittent software fault which meant that his speedometer occasionally gave incorrect readings. This was quickly fixed by the garage, who commented on how unusual it was for this make and model to have any problems at all. Unfortunately, some months later, Jack was driving along an unfamiliar, relatively empty road when the fault occurred again. He had, however, no reason to doubt the speedometer and as there were no cars in front of him to give clues about his speed, he inadvertently drove at 15 miles over the 40 miles per hour limit. Unfortunately for Jack, he was being followed by a police car and was pulled over and issued with a ticket. Jack felt hard done by because he had no intention to break the law and, as he honestly believed at the time of the offence that he was driving at the right speed, he chose to defend the case and go to court. However, Jack lost his case because the prosecutor argued that speedometers are only intended as indications of speed and that Jack should have been aware from the feel of the car and clues from the external environment that he was driving too fast. Jack was found guilty and had to accept the consequences of a fine and points on his licence.

However, that was not the end of the story because the magistrates were not the only people investigating the case. The road safety officer from the local council was interested in understanding more about why an experienced and skilled driver like Jack had become so dependent on the speedometer that he had failed to notice the other clues to his speed and had as a consequence committed a potentially dangerous offence. He also wanted to understand how new drivers were taught and encouraged (if indeed they were) to monitor their speed using methods other than their speedometers. This investigation was not about establishing blame (that had already been done by the court), it was about learning from Jack's experience and sharing the learning with others to change driver behaviour and improve road safety. The road safety officer talked to Jack to find out more about what he was thinking and experiencing at the time of the offence. He also talked to the police and local driving instructors to find out more about driver training, education and the skills that could be used to judge the speed that a car was travelling at. He then used the information gained to work with a local paper to mount a joint campaign to raise awareness of the issue and encourage drivers to use their skills and judgement in conjunction with the speedometer to regulate their driving speed.

Although there are big differences between social work and driving a car, there are some clear parallels between the two. Both involve high-risk decision making in situations where there is a complex and rapidly changing interaction between an operator, tools and the environment. In both, routine practice and over-dependence on tools and procedures can get in the way of the use of skilled judgement and of taking personal responsibility for actions. In the car example, Jack had become so dependent on the speedometer that he failed to see the need to use the skills, knowledge and judgement he had gained from years of driving experience. Jack told the road safety officer that when he reflected back, his gut instinct had been that he was driving too fast but that he remembered checking the speedometer and dismissing his concerns because he had absolute faith in the reliability of his still relatively new car (after all, the marketing spiel and the mechanic had told him it was the most reliable car in the world!). Understanding why this dependence had developed and how easily the evidence that informed Jack's gut instinct had been dismissed in the face of so-called reliable evidence helped the road safety officer plan a campaign aimed at other drivers to change their attitudes and improve their driving behaviours. The error Jack made with his speed could have led to a serious or even fatal accident. In social work, unwanted consequences and even deaths have occurred in high-profile cases because of a similar over-dependence on procedure and lack of application of professional judgement (Munro, 2011).

In the driving example, we have shown that if we want driving safety standards to improve, we need not just to establish that an offence had been committed but also to understand why Jack thought and acted as he did. Similarly, in professional practice, if we want to do more than identify what went wrong in a particular situation, we need to understand the complex and multi-faceted system that the practitioners were working in at the time. This includes understanding what they were thinking and feeling at the time and how this influenced their decision making. It is only by achieving this level of understanding that useful lessons can be learned that will help avoid similar errors in the future and result in improvements in safeguarding practice.

Systems-based case review processes enable participants to go beyond establishing a sequence of events and help them to develop an understanding of why

> *actions or decisions that later turn out to be mistakes or led to an unwanted outcome, seemed to those involved, to be the sensible thing to do at the time.*

(SCIE, 2012)

The serious case review process is designed to uncover the thoughts and feelings of those involved and seeks to gain an understanding of the situation as if seen through their eyes. The Social Care Institute for Excellence (SCIE) has produced a set of detailed guidance for people responsible for leading and participating in serious case reviews with materials available on its website: **www.scie.org.uk**. These materials are useful for anyone involved in a serious case review but can also be adapted and used by managers who wish to adopt a systems approach to routine case reviews within their organisation. Table 13.1 outlines the serious case review process.

Table 13.1 The serious case review process (based on SCIE, 2012)

	Serious case review process
Preparation	Identifying a case for review Selecting the review team Identifying who should be involved, i.e. key stake-holders in the case Preparing participants
Data collection	Selecting relevant documentation/records One-to-one conversations/structured interviews with participants
Organising and analysing data	Producing a narrative of multi-agency perspectives arising from the interviews Identifying and recording key practice episodes and their contributory factors Reviewing the data and analysis Identifying and prioritising generic patterns Making recommendations

Why does the systems approach lead to a more critical understanding of a case?

The SCIE model involves drawing on evidence from documents such as case records but crucially places a strong emphasis on the information gained from facilitated conversations with front-line practitioners with an involvement in the case under review. It provides a template to guide discussions that enable practitioners to:

- provide an overview of the case;

- identify turning points;

- critically explore and explain their mindset;

- critically explore factors that influenced their interpretation of the situation and the actions that they took;

- identify things that went well;

- make suggestions for change;

- reflect on the process and outcomes of the conversation.

The model makes use of critical questioning (Brookfield, 1987; Fook and Gardner, 2007) to encourage and support honest and in-depth reflection on the circumstances surrounding the case. The facilitator's role is to uncover the thoughts and feelings of the practitioners but also to ask questions that provoke deeper and more critical analysis and evaluation. The process encourages practitioners to identify sources of bias and uncover any assumptions made by them that influenced their perception of the situation or the actions that they took at the time.

Another crucial dimension of the systems approach to serious case reviews is the viewpoint that individual workers' practice is a result of both their own skill and knowledge and the wider organisational setting in which they are working. The approach identifies the variables that constitute this wider context and takes them into account in its analysis. Figure 13.1 identifies some of the key variables.

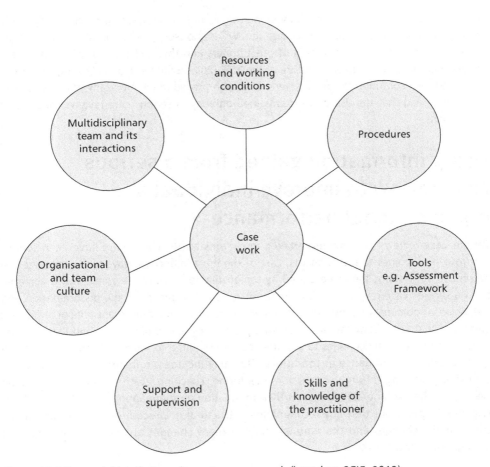

Figure 13.1 Key variables that can impact on case work (based on SCIE, 2012).

ACTIVITY **13.1**

Organisational cultures and serious case reviews

Refer back to the first section of the book to remind yourself about links between organisational culture, critical reflection and learning. What impact do you think organisational culture will have on the processes and outcomes of serious case reviews?

People do not just critically reflect because they are asked to do so (Moon, 1999) and the conditions in which individuals function will have an impact on the quality of their reflection. People who feel unsafe and undervalued and who believe that change is unlikely are less likely to reflect honestly and critically, and are much less likely to share their reflections with others. In the first section of the book we explored the importance of developing and sustaining a culture that supports learning. Serious case reviews need to be seen by people at all levels within organisations as an opportunity to learn and to make changes and not as a threatening experience. This is only likely to happen in an organisation which has a culture that genuinely supports and values learning and with processes that ensure that learning is shared.

Another consideration is avoiding blaming individuals but rather seeing problems as systemic. The approach also means that serious case reviews are not solely based on the views of senior managers. Constructive engagement of practitioners and their willingness to reflect on and analyse their practice has been a feature of the SCIE (2012) pilot work and allowing all workers to see and then contribute to the final report has also proved to be important. The government has now agreed that the use of a systems methodology in serious case reviews should be a requirement.

Using information gained from a serious case review to improve individual and organisational performance

Serious case reviews are only undertaken in circumstances when there have been serious unforeseen outcomes to involvements. One of the most important ways that a message can be sent to staff about the value placed by senior managers on the learning that is achieved from a serious case review is for a structure to be put in place for the dissemination and discussion of outcomes, at individual, team, organisational and interorganisational levels. It is important that any recommendations made by the review are implemented and that staff are supported to make any changes to practice that are required to improve both individual and organisational performance in the future. This may include augmenting, reinforcing and embedding learning through supervision, mentoring, coaching, team meetings and training events (see the relevant chapters for further information on these approaches). In parallel it is also clearly important that any recommended structural or procedural changes are made, and that the changes and the rationale behind these changes are clearly communicated throughout the organisation.

How can case reviews be used in everyday practice?

Research into pilot studies applying the SCIE systems approach to serious case reviews has indicated that learning outcomes are improved and that the process is valued by participants (Fish *et al.*, 2010). Munro (2011) has suggested that social care agencies would benefit from including case reviews as a routine part of practice to ensure that services are user- and carer-centred and that practitioners continuously develop their professional capability. Case reviews can be used flexibly within organisations to provide an opportunity for workers to critically review and evaluate both individual and organisational practice.

Whilst the approach could be used to explore 'near misses', i.e. cases where a serious incident was only narrowly avoided, Munro (2011) has suggested that they could also be valuable in situations where everything has gone well. Learning from success allows an organisation to build on its strengths and transfer good practice to other situations.

The problem with the full serious case review methodology outlined in Table 13.1 is that it is a major piece of social research and is very time-consuming, and is based on the availability of a facilitator or facilitators. However, as its essence is the critical analysis of practice from a systems perspective, it could be used less intensively. So, for instance, case reviews can be seen as a valuable way of augmenting supervision in that, whilst a supervisor is seen to have a role in identifying quality problems and then 'mediating' with the wider organisation to bring improvement (see Chapter 7), this depends on an analysis of the problem to identify possible causes. A case review would facilitate this, so one could see a supervisor and supervisee taking a particular case and reviewing it together in depth, using the critical questions outlined below. The problem with this is that it does not involve the wider multidisciplinary team and draw on their perspectives.

However, case reviews could be held that involve people who work together within a team, or people from different services who are working with a particular service user or group of service users. At its most basic, a case review is a forum at which knowledge can be shared, options discussed and actions reviewed. In addition, if facilitated effectively, a case review can provide the opportunity for members of the participating group to challenge each other's assumptions, uncover alternative perspectives and critically explore a range of explanations and alternative actions. Case reviews would provide social workers and other allied professionals with a process that can help them to understand better complex cases, support decision making and enable learning. They could be used not only to explore cases that are problematic but also to highlight and share effective, creative and innovative practice (Munro, 2011).

Case reviews could be incorporated into existing meetings such as team or interprofessional forums (where the case review would be one agenda item), or can be convened specifically for the purpose of reviewing complex, problematic or interesting cases. Some organisations hold case review meetings regularly (once a month or even more frequently) whilst others convene review meetings when the need arises for a more in-depth exploration of a case or cases. A case review could also provide a very good basis for a group supervision session.

Managers or workers normally put forward cases for discussion and it will generally be the worker who is taking a lead in a case that will prepare and present initial background information to the meeting. As a manager you can play an important role in instigating, co-ordinating and supporting the process of case review, although a facilitator could be another team manager or a practitioner not involved in the case. As highlighted earlier, the process needs to be supported by a widespread and embedded culture for learning, which managers at all levels in organisations should be part of promoting, developing and maintaining. Modelling a commitment to open enquiry and critically reflective practice is a fundamental part of your role as a professional manager in the health and social care sector.

An interesting issue is the extent to which people who use services might be involved in a case review. Their perspective could only be seen as invaluable and in a truly participative service one could see a case review as being centred on them and their experiences. This would need to be handled sensitively and there could be difficulties with confidentiality. However, the service user might be well aware of the members of the multidisciplinary team and their views through formal case-planning meetings so this might not prove to be problematic. Crucially, their views on how their case has been managed and the outcomes for them need to be at the centre of a case review.

Taking a systems approach to routine case reviews

Similar stages, outlined in the previous section on serious case reviews, can be applied in routine case reviews to provide a structure for preparation and discussion and to support critical analysis and evaluation. An overview of the case can be prepared and presented by a worker or small group of workers most closely involved with the case. The wider group can then support the process by the use of critical questioning to:

- *identify turning points;*
- *critically explore and explain the mindset of the workers;*
- *critically explore factors that influenced their interpretation of the situation and the actions that they took;*
- *identify things that went well;*
- *make suggestions for change.*

(Brookfield, 1987; Fook and Gardner, 2007)

Communal agreement of the analysis and the recommendations that are developed gives them validity. A case review approach also does much to facilitate any changes generated as they will be owned from the outset by the practitioners themselves.

ACTIVITY **13.2**

Facilitating case reviews

How could case reviews be used routinely in your organisation? Who do you think would be the best person to organise and facilitate a case review in your organisation/team? What benefits and disadvantages are there to having a facilitator who is not a line manager of people involved in a case review?

Embedding the learning from case reviews

The case review process can be an important starting point for enabling learning from complex and problematic cases. Undertaking the review can foster critical reflection and encourage learning that can lead to both changes in individual practice and to organisational policies and procedures. However, to ensure that key learning from the review process is not lost, it is vital that it is seen as part of a joined-up organisational learning and development strategy and not as something which will effect change in isolation. Learning from the review needs to be disseminated beyond the group of participants (to policy makers and managers as well as to workers engaged in similar or related practice), although senior managers with responsibility for service quality and performance might welcome the opportunity to be part of the review as a way of developing a better understanding of practice for which they are responsible, but from which they are inevitably distanced. Opportunities need to be provided for individual learning to be reinforced, developed and embedded through, for example, supervision, mentoring, coaching, team meetings and training opportunities.

FURTHER READING

Fook, J. and Gardner, F. (2007) *Practising Critical Reflection: A resource handbook.* Maidenhead: McGraw Hill/OU Press.

SCIE (2012). At a glance 01: Learning together to safeguard children: a 'systems' model for case reviews. Available from: www.scie.org.uk/publications/ataglance/ataglance01.asp

The Social Care Institute for Excellence (SCIE) (www.scie.org.uk) has a wide range of resources on its website that will be useful for anyone involved in a serious case review or wanting to use a systems approach in routine case reviews. This includes guides to practice, a training video, reports on pilot studies and evaluations of the approach.

References

ACAS (2001) *Effective Organisations: The people factor.* London: ACAS.

Adair, J. (1983) *Effective Leadership.* London: Pan.

Adams, R., Dominelli, L. and Payne, M. (eds) (2009) *Critical Practice in Social Work* (2nd edn). London: Palgrave.

Advocacy in Action (2006) Making it our own ball game: Learning and assessment in social work education. *Social Work Education*, 25(4): 332–346.

Argyris, C. and Schön, D. (1978) *Organizational Learning: A theory of action perspective.* Reading, MA: Addison Wesley.

Armstrong, M. (2006) *Performance Management: Key strategies and practical guidelines.* London: Kogan Page.

Atherton, J.S. (2011a) *Doceo: Learning as loss 1.* Available from: www.doceo.co.uk/original/learnloss_1.htm

Atherton, J.S. (2011b) *Teaching and Learning: Advance organisers.* Available from: www.learningand teaching.info/teaching/advance_organisers.htm

Barnett, R. and Coate, K. (2005) *Engaging the Curriculum in Higher Education.* Maidenhead: Open University Press.

Beddoe, L. (2009) Creating continuous conversation: social workers and learning organisations. *Social Work Education*, 28(7): 722–736.

Beresford, P. and Boxall, K. (2012) Service users, social work education and knowledge for social work practice. *Social Work Education*, 31(2): 155–167.

Beverley, A. and Worsley, A. (2007) *Learning and Teaching in Social Work Practice.* London: Palgrave Macmillan.

Biggs, J. (1999) What the student does: teaching for enhanced learning. *Higher Education Research and Development*, 18(1): 57–75.

Boud, D., Keogh, R. and Walker, D. (1985) *Reflection: Turning experience into learning.* London: Croom Helm.

Boud, D., Cressey, P. and Docherty, P. (2006) *Productive Reflection at Work.* London: Routledge.

Brookfield, S. (1987) *Developing Critical Thinkers.* San Francisco, CA: Jossey Bass.

Brown, L.M. and Pozner, B.Z. (2001) Exploring the relationship between learning and leadership. *Leadership and Organisational Development Journal*, 22(6): 274–280.

Carey, M. (2009) Happy shopper? The problem with service user and carer participation. *British Journal of Social Work*, 39(1): 179–188.

CCNAP (2001) *Asking the Experts: A guide to involving people in shaping health and social care service.* Community Care Needs Assessment Project (CCNAP). Grimsby: North East Lincolnshire Primary Care Trust.

Cherry, N. (2005) Preparing for practice in the age of complexity. *Higher Education Research and Development*, 24(4): 309–320.

Chrusciel, D. and Field, D.W. (2006) Success factors in dealing with significant change in an organisation. *Business Process Management*, 12(4): 503–516.

CIPD (2011) *Coaching and Mentoring Factsheet*. Available from: http://www.cipd.co.uk/hr-resources/factsheets/coaching-mentoring.aspx

Clapton, G., Cree, V., Allan, M., Edwards, R., Forbes, R., Irwin, M., Paterson, W. and Perry, R. (2006) Grasping the nettle: integrating learning and practice revisited and re-imagined. *Social Work Education*, 25(6): 645–656.

Coffield, F., Moseley, D., Hall, E. and Ecclestone, K. (2004) *Learning Styles and Pedagogy in Post-16 Learning: A systematic and critical review*. London: Learning Skills Research Centre (now LSN).

Connor, M. and Pokora, J. (2007) *Coaching and Mentoring at Work*. Buckingham: Open University Press.

Connor, M. and Pokora, J. (2012) *Coaching and Mentoring at Work: Developing effective practice* (2nd edn). London: McGraw Hill/OU Press.

Cooper, B. (2008) Continuing professional development: a critical approach. In: Fraser, S. and Matthews, S. (eds) *The Critical Practitioner in Social Work and Health Care*. London: Sage: 222–237.

Csikszentmihalyi, M. (1988) The flow experience and its significance for human psychology. In: Csikszentmihalyi, M. and Csikszentmihalyi, I.S. (eds) *Optimal Experience: Psychological studies of flow in consciousness*. Cambridge: Cambridge University Press: 15–35.

Csikszentmihalyi, M. (1990) *Flow: The psychology of optimal experience*. New York: Harper and Row.

Csikszentmihalyi, M. (2008) *What Makes a Life Worth Living*. Available from: http://uk.youtube.com/watch?v=fXIeFJCqsPs

Davys, A. and Beddoe, L. (2009) The reflective learning model: supervision of social work students. *Social Work Education*, 28(8): 919–933.

DoH (2002a) *Focus on the Future: Key messages from the focus groups about the future of social work training*. London: HMSO.

DoH (2002b) *Requirements for Social Work Training*. London: HMSO.

DoH (2006) *Our Health, Our Care, Our Say: A new direction for community services*. London: HMSO.

Doel, M., Sawdon, C. and Morrison, D. (2002) *Learning, Practice and Assessment*. London: Jessica Kingsley.

Duffy, J. (2008) *Looking Out from the Middle: User involvement in health and social care in Northern Ireland*. London: SCIE.

Festinger, L. (1957) *A Theory of Cognitive Dissonance*. Stanford, CA: Stanford University Press.

Fish, S. and Munro, E. (2008) *Learning Together to Safeguard Children: Developing a multi agency systems approach for case reviews*. SCIE report 19. Available from: www.scie.org.uk/publications/reports/report19.asp

Fish, S., Munro, E. and Bairstow, S. (2010) *Piloting the SCIE Systems Model for Case Reviews: Learning from the north west*. Final report. Available from: www.scie.org.uk/children/learningtogether/files/NWPilotsReport.pdf

Flynn, N. (2002) *Public Sector Management*. Harlow: Prentice Hall.

Fook, J. and Gardner, F. (2007) *Practising Critical Reflection: A resource handbook*. Maidenhead: McGraw Hill/OU Press.

Fook, J., Ryan, M. and Hawkins, L. (2000) *Professional Expertise: Practice, theory and education for working in uncertainty*. London: Whiting and Birch.

Gould, N. and Baldwin, M. (2004) *Social Work, Critical Reflection and the Learning Organisation*. Aldershot: Ashgate.

Gray, I., Parker, J., Rutter, L. and Williams, S. (2010a) Developing communities of practice: effective leadership, management and supervision in social work. *Social Work and Social Sciences Review*, 14(2): 20–36.

Gray, I., Field, R. and Brown, K. (2010b) *Effective Leadership, Management and Supervision in Health and Social Care*. Exeter: Learning Matters.

GSCC (2005) *The Revised Post Qualifying Framework for Social Work Education and Training*. Available from: www.gscc.org.uk

Hafford-Letchfield, T., Leonard, K., Begum, N. and Chick, N. (2008) *Leadership and Management in Social Care*. London: Sage.

Handy, C. (1993) *Understanding Organisations*. London: Penguin.

Hanley, B., Bradburn, J., Barnes, M., Evans, C., Goodare, H., Kelson, M., Kent, A., Oliver, S., Thomas, S. and Wallcraft, J. (2003) *Involving the Public in NHS, Public Health and Social Care Research: Briefing notes for researchers* (2nd edn). London: INVOLVE.

Hastings, M. (2000) User involvement in education and training. In: Pierce, R. and Weinstein, J. (eds) *Innovative Education and Training for Care Professionals. A provider's guide*. London: Jessica Kingsley: 97–110.

Hefferman, K. (2006) Does language make a difference in health and social care practice? Exploring the new language of the service user in the United Kingdom. *International Social Work*, 49: 825–830.

Hock, D. (2000) *The Art of Chaordic Leadership. Leader to Leader, No. 15. The Peter F. Drucker Foundation for Nonprofit Management*. Available from: www.hesselbeininstitute.org/knowledgecenter/journal.aspx?ArticleID=62

Joy-Mathews, J., Megginson, D. and Surtees, M. (2004) *Human Resource Development*. London: Kogan Page.

Kadushin, A. (1976) *Supervision in Social Work*. New York: Columbia University Press.

Kadushin, A. and Harkness, D. (2002) *Supervision in Social Work* (4th edn). New York: Columbia University Press.

Knott, C. and Scragg, T. (2007) *Reflective Practice in Social Work*. Exeter: Learning Matters.

Knowles, M. (1980) *The Modern Practice of Adult Education: From pedagogy to andragogy* (2nd edn). Englewood Cliffs, NJ: Prentice Hall/Cambridge.

Knowles, M. (1990) *The Adult Learner: A neglected species* (4th edn). London: Gulf Publishers.

Kolb, D.A. (1984) *Experiential Learning: Experience as the source of learning and development*. Englewood Cliffs, NJ: Prentice Hall.

Kotter, J.P. (1996) *Leading Change.* Boston, MA: Harvard Business School Press.

Lave, J. and Wenger, E. (1991) *Situated Learning, Legitimate Peripheral Participation.* Cambridge: Cambridge University Press.

Lawlor, J. and Bilson, A. (2010) *Social Work Management and Leadership: Managing complexity with creativity.* London: Taylor and Francis.

Lowes, L. and Hullatt, I. (eds) (2005) *Involving Service Users in Health and Social Care Research.* London: Routledge

Mabey, C. (2001) *Preparing for Change: Context and choice. Block 3, Managing change.* Buckingham: Open University Press.

McGregor, D. (1957) An uneasy look at performance appraisal. *Harvard Business Review,* May-June: 89–94.

McGregor, D. (2005) *The Human Side of Enterprise.* New York: McGraw-Hill.

Mainiero, L.A. and Sullivan, S.E. (2005) Kaleidoscope careers: an alternative explanation for the opt-out generation. *Academy of Management Executive,* 19(1): 106–123.

Marton, F. and Saljo, R. (1976) On qualitative differences in learning: 1. Outcome and process. *British Journal of Educational Psychology,* 46: 4–11.

Miettinen, R. (2000) The concept of experiential learning and John Dewey's theory of reflective thought and action. *International Journal of Lifelong Education,* 19(1): 54–72.

Moon, J. (1999) *Reflection in Learning and Professional Development: Theory and practice.* London: Kogan Page.

Moriarty, J., Rapaport, P., Beresford, P., Fran Branfield, F., Forrest, V., Manthorpe, J., Martineau, S., Cornes, M., Butt, J., Iliffe, S., Taylor, B. and Keady, J. (2007) *Practice Guide: The participation of adult service users, including older people, in developing social care.* Stakeholder Participation SCIE Guide 17. London: SCIE.

Mullins, L.J. (2005) *Management and Organisational Behaviour.* Harlow: Prentice Hall.

Mullins L.J. (2007) *Management and Organisational Behaviour* (2nd edn). Harlow: Pearson.

Munro, E. (2011) *The Munro Review of Child Protection: The final report – a child centred system.* London: Department for Education.

Neary, M. (2000) *Teaching, Assessing and Evaluation for Clinical Competence.* Cheltenham: Nelson Thornes.

Nixon, S. and Murr, A. (2006) Practice learning and the development of professional practice. *Social Work Education,* 25(8): 798–811.

O'Sullivan, J. (2006) Continuing professional development. In: Jones, R. and Jenkins, F. (eds) *Developing the Allied Health Professional.* Abingdon: Radcliffe: 1–16.

Plaskoff, J. (2006) Intersubjectivity and community building: learning to learn organisationally. In: Easterby-Smith, M. and Lyles, M.A. (eds) *Handbook of Organizational Learning and Knowledge Management.* Oxford: Blackwell.

Pritchard, J. (ed.) (1995) *Good Practice in Supervision.* London: Jessica Kingsley.

Race, P. (2010) *Making Learning Happen* (2nd edn). London: Sage.

Robert Gordon University (c. 2008) *Leading Change: A guide for managers*. Available from: www4.rgu.ac.uk/files/A%20quick%20look%20guide%20to%20leading%20change.PPT#22

Robson, P., Sampson, A.S., Dime, N., Hernandez, L. and Litherland, R. (2008) *Seldom Heard: Developing inclusive participation in social care*. Adults' Services Position Paper 10. London: SCIE.

Rogers, A. (2002) *Teaching Adults*. Maidenhead: OU Press.

Rolfe, G., Freshwater, D. and Jasper, M. (2001) *Critical Reflection for Nursing*. Basingstoke: Palgrave.

Rutter, L. and Brown, K. (2012) *Critical Thinking and Professional Judgement for Social Work*. Exeter: Learning Matters.

Sadd, J. (2011) *'We Are More Than Our Story': Service user and carer participation in social work education*. SCIE Report 42. London: SCIE.

Schön, D.A. (1992) *The Reflective Practitioner*. San Francisco, CA: Jossey-Bass.

Senge, P.M. (1990) *The Fifth Discipline: The art and practice of a learning organisation*. London: Random House.

SCIE (2012) *At a Glance 01: Learning together to safeguard children: a systems model for case reviews*. Available from: www.scie.org.uk/publications/ataglance/ataglance01.asp

Shaping Our Lives (2007) *Developing Social Care: Service users driving culture change*. People management knowledge review 17. London: SCIE.

Skills for Care England (2004) *Leadership and Management: A strategy for the social care workforce*. Leeds: TOPSS.

SWRB (2010) *Building a Safe and Confident Future: One year on*. London: Social Work Reform Board.

SWRB (2011) *Standards for Employers and Supervision Framework Statement*. Available from: www.education.gov.uk/swrb/social/a0074240/professional-standards-for-social-workers-in-england

SWTF (2009) *Building a Safe, Confident Future. The final report of the social work task force: November 2009*. London: SWTF.

Taylor, C. and White, S. (2006) Knowledge and reasoning in social work: educating for humane judgement. *British Journal of Social Work*, 36(2): 189–206.

Thompson, N. (2000) *Theory and Practice in Human Service* (2nd edn). Buckingham: OU Press.

Thompson, N. (2006) *Promoting Workplace Learning*. Bristol: Policy Press.

Thompson, S. and Thompson, N. (2008) *The Critically Reflective Practitioner*. Basingstoke: Palgrave Macmillan.

Tsui, M.S. (2005) *Social Work Supervision: Contexts and concepts*. London: Sage.

Tyler, G. (2006) Addressing barriers to participation: service user involvement in social work training. *Social Work Education*, 25(4): 385–392.

Tyreman, S. (2000) Promoting critical thinking in health care: phronesis and criticality. *Medicine, Health Care and Philosophy*, 3: 117–124.

Vakola, M. and Nikolaou, I. (2005) Attitudes towards organizational change. What is the role of employees' stress and commitment? *Employee Relations*, 27(2): 160–174.

Vygotsky, L.S. (1986) *Thought and Language* (translated by Kozulin, A.). Cambridge: MIT Press.

Walker, J., Crawford, K. and Parker, J. (2008) *Practice Education in Social Work: A handbook for practice teachers, assessors and educators.* Exeter: Learning Matters.

Wenger, E. (1998) *Communities of Practice: Learning, meaning and identity.* Cambridge: Cambridge University Press.

Wenger, E. (2006) *Communities of Practice In and Across the 21st Century Organisation.* Available from: www.ewenger.com/pub/pubpapers.htm

Wenger, E., McDermott, R. and Snyder, W. (2002) *Cultivating Communities of Practice: A guide to managing knowledge.* Harvard, MA: Harvard Business School Press.

Williams, S. and Rutter, L. (2010) *The Practice Educator's Handbook.* Exeter: Learning Matters.

Winter, R. and Maisch, M. (1996) *Professional Competence and Higher Education: The ASET programme.* London: Falmer Press.

Wright, P., Turner, C., Clay, D. and Mills, H. (2006) *Participation of Children and Young People in Developing Social Care.* Practice guide 2006. London: Social Care Institute for Excellence.

Index